Alicorn.
19.

UNICORN

All, all in Life's but repetition,
Fancy sole is new in ev'ry stage.
What in past days nowhere came to vision,
That alone doth never age!

Friedrich von Schiller
From: *To My Friends*

UNICORN
Myth and Reality

Rüdiger Robert Beer
Translated by Charles M. Stern

VNR VAN NOSTRAND REINHOLD COMPANY
New York Cincinnati Toronto London Melbourne

A James J Kery Book

Library of Congress Catalog Card Number 77-8173
ISBN 0-442-80583-7

Printed in the United States of America.

Published by Van Nostrand Reinhold Company
A division of Litton Educational Publishing, Inc.
135 West 50th Street, New York, NY 10020, U.S.A.

Van Nostrand Reinhold Limited
1410 Birchmount Road
Scarborough, Ontario M1P 2E7, Canada

Van Nostrand Reinhold Australia Pty. Ltd.
17 Queen Street
Mitcham, Victoria 3132, Australia

Van Nostrand Reinhold Company Limited
Molly Millars Lane
Workingham, Berkshire, England

16 15 14 13 12 11 10 9 8 7 6 5 4 3 2

Library of Congress Cataloging in Publication Data
Beer, Rudiger Robert.

    Unicorn.
Translation of Einhorn: Fabelwelt und Wirklichkeit
    Bibliography: p.
    Includes index.
    I. Unicorns.   I. Title.
GR830.U6B4413 700 77-8173

The Author tenders his sincerest thanks to those many friends
whose suggestions and advice have for more than a decade
fostered and encouraged his researches on the Unicorn.

Originally published in West Germany 1972 as
Einhorn: Fabelwelt und Wirklichkeit
© 1972 Verlag Georg D. W. Callwey, Munchen

Der Silberdistelwald aus Gedichte—Oskar Loerke
© S. Fischer Verlag GmbH, Frankfurt am Main, 1954
Einhorn-aus Heir-Hilde Domin © S. Fisher Verlag GmbH
Frankfurt am Main, 1954

The poem Unicorn Hunt by Eckart Klessmann was quoted
by kind permission of the author. The original is from the
volume of poetry Einhornjagd (Unicorn Hunt), Stuttgart,
1963.

The jacket illustration is a woodcut
taken from Tierbuch (Animal Book),
by Michael Herr, Strassburg, 1546.

Contents

1. A Fascinating Figment

O, here's the beast that no existence hath.

Rainer Maria Rilke, *Sonnets to Orpheus,* pt. 2

THE UNICORN is as old as the knowledge of ancient China and still appears in contemporary literature, but it has never actually roamed the earth. It is a creature which never existed but has nonetheless fascinated man for thousands of years.

In childhood we learn about unicorns; for many of us, our first encounter with the beast may be through the fairy tale of the bold little tailor who had to fulfill three tasks to gain the hand of the princess. One of those tasks was to catch a unicorn which was devastating her father's realm. With axe and rope in hand, the tailor enters the forest, provokes the beast, and at the crucial moment jumps behind a tree. The infuriated animal charges, rams the trunk with his horn, and thus becomes helpless to evade the rope by which the tailor will lead him to the king. The idea of trapping the creature by such a rugged method predates any European tale; from time immemorial the lion used similar ruses in his legendary battles with the unicorn. There is, as we shall see, a neater and more clever way of overcoming the unicorn, but in any case, it was always the king who had prior claim to the spoil; unicorn hunting was indeed a royal prerogative.

The creature of fable is very much with us outside of books too. The German poet Christian Morgenstern is wrong in his contention that the unicorn survives "only on tavern signboards." You can, for example, today buy your medicine at scores of "Unicorn" pharmacies in Western Europe and elsewhere. Before house numbers came into use, dwellings were frequently identified by animal names, and anyone setting up a business, say a tavern or printing house, accordingly took over the original name and sign. Through their relationship to the evangelists, symbols such as the bull, eagle, and lion had some religious connotation, as did the unicorn. Apothecaries without doubt were particularly happy to acquire the unicorn symbol, for it had gained both a spiritual and medical significance.

In many a church, the elegant beast is present in the coats of arms or crests of tombstone escutcheons. In still more houses of worship, it is present in the words of the service. *Libera me de ore leonis: et a cornibus unicornium humilitatem meam* says Psalm 21 of the Palm Sunday tract in the Roman missal; it is rendered in the vernacular as "Deliver me from the lion's mouth: and my lowliness from the horns of unicorns." In the King

1. Three-inch tall ibex, Persian, middle of second century B.C.

James version this is Psalm 22:21, "Save me from the lion's mouth: for thou has heard me from the horns of the unicorns," but in modern Protestant versions the animal is weakened to a wild beast or wild ox. This was the psalm recited by Christ on the cross. If your eyes are sharp enough, you can spot him in sacred precincts and in museums more frequently than you might imagine. The unicorn is clearly something greater than a mere curiosity. What *is* it then?

The image of the unicorn has evolved variously in the cultures of mankind. Although nobody knows for certain, it presumably reached Europe from the ranges and plains of India, travelling along three more or less parallel routes until these contracted, intersected, and merged. It originally appeared as a literary creation; pictorial representation came later. The first route of the unicorn was through the classical antiquity of the Greeks and Romans, the second through the Bible, and the third through an early Christian manuscript on natural history, the *Physiologus,* or "Natural Philosopher," which also emanated from the Near East. We shall be delving further into each of these routes as well as following the journey of the fabulous beast through Western civilization, even to its ramifications in America.

The physical form of the animal varies little in the representations we can ordinarily discover around us: an equine body, cloven hooves, often a goatee, always the long, tapering, spiraling horn. But once this was not the case. Occasionally he bore some resemblance to a kid, ram, or stag. His horn did not always point straight up or forward but sometimes curved backward either gently or in a bold arc; it was even shown sometimes as growing from the nose. But this did not make a rhinoceros out of him. Nevertheless, in medieval literature the terms unicorn and rhinoceros were often synonymous. At times the unicorn was described as large as a mountain, or small enough for a damsel to fondle in her lap. Sometimes it was hybrid, a combination of parts from various species. Since it had a special association with water in both a medical and religious sense, it was occasionally given the tail of a fish. And in Asia, the unicorn sprouted wings. Nor has its coloration remained constant; it developed from white, as described in ancient reports, to the yellow of boxwood, and later to the brownness of a stag. In its latest, noblest, almost overrefined form it regained its dazzling white of the fairytale era. In modern novels the unicorn sometimes turns up as a female despite the inherent maleness of the beast. Perhaps this is a reverberation of its grammatically female character in some languages (as *la licorne* in French).

Predominant in accounts of the unicorn are the practical qualities of the animal's horn as an effective antidote and cure-all. (Hence the significance of the unicorn in pharmacies.) Naturally it is tempting to imagine the unicorn's horn as belonging in the alchemist's armamentarium. The mystics could scarcely ignore that magical token which penetrated esoteric cabals such as the Rosicrucians. The horn was a treasured love potion and even today represents an aphrodisiac, although chamois horn is now its accepted substitute. From the very beginning, the unicorn appeared everywhere as a symbol of fertility, potency, and trenchant virility. The phallic symbolism of the horn persists even in later ecclesiological evolutions of the myth.

The unicorn was viewed coolly and scientifically by the ancients. Its diverse, protean, symbolic, and mystic meaning came essentially from Christianity. At a very early date, it became an ideograph for Christ, yet it stood also for Death and the Devil; in this last case Asiatic influences were powerfully at work. The unicorn represented the all-conquering power of the Lord, yet at the same time it stood for meekness clad in the sinful garb of mankind. It could be incorporated into armorial bearings as a sign of knightly courage but might equally well symbolize monastic seclusion. Becoming associated with the Virgin through the Son of Man, the unicorn was, further, a symbol of chastity. But because of its boundless strength it also embodied unlimited licentiousness: the horn as aphrodisiac in yet another guise. The contradictory nature of the creature is manifold. It could symbolize Christians and the unity of the Church as well as their adversaries, Jew or Gentile. In the Middle Ages it could play two roles – one deadly earnest, the other loutish buffoonery. Myth brings with it ambiguity. In man's primordial consciousness, the divine verges on the sinister. Take the Latin word *sacer*, for example; both "holy" and "accursed" are among its meanings. And though the lion symbolizes Christ's sovereignty, the devil, too, roams like a roaring lion.

The age of Romance and of nineteenth-century symbolic art made use of the beast in a rather contrived manner. This seems true also for those speculations which retrospectively interpreted the lion and the unicorn as a coupled symbol for the sun and the moon. Right through to the present day, the unicorn has been a stimulus to the arts, both fine and applied, to painting and sculpture, poetry and music. In the words of the German writer Gustav René Hocke, it is one of the most fascinating, protean symbols in the European history of ideas.

The fabulous beast will elude any investigator who is informed solely by reason, by his personal modern education and acquired knowledge. No, to give the unicorn his due, one must try to put aside prejudice and become steeped instead in the innocence and credulity of the centuries of men and women who took the manifold forms of the beast in all seriousness. Only then is one rewarded in the pursuit and only then does one sense that the unicorn enjoyed a high degree of reality – and possibly still does! For the unicorn is not a creature of logic.

2. Virgin and unicorn from *Hortus sanitatis* (Garden of Health), Mainz fifteenth century

3. Chapter opening from Albertus
Magnus's bestiary *Summa de creaturis*
(German edition, 1545)

Von der Natur / art vnnd eygen=

schafft der Thier / welcher namen anfahet inn

frembden sprachen / darmit sie vonn den alten ge ∙
nant worden am Buchstaben V.

Vnicornis ein Einhorn.

Vnicornis ein Einhorn / ist bei vns ein frembd vnbekandt thier / zim∙
licher grösse / doch gegē seiner treflichen sterckɛ zu rechnen / nit groß von leib /
von farben gelbfarb wie buxbaumen holtz / hat gespalten kloen / wonet im
gebſtrg vñ hohen wildtnussen / hat vornen an der stirn ein seht lang scharpff
horn / welches es an den felsen vnd steinen scherpffet / durchsticht darmit die
H iij   grossen

2. Reports from the East

Its body, at least as big as a horse, was white. It had a scarlet head and startlingly blue eyes. Its horn was a cubit long, white at the base, black in the middle, blood-red at the tip. This was the Indian wild ass – the first single-horned beast to appear in European geography and natural science.

As extraordinary as its coloring was its fleetness of foot. Because of the ever-increasing momentum of its speed when pursued, the only way to capture the animal was by encircling herds as the elder beasts led foals to pasture. Instead of dashing for safety, the sires would fight with horn, hoof, and jaws, costing the lives of many a horse and rider, although they succumbed finally to the superior force of bows and arrows. [Ill. 4]

What could be so precious that men were willing to expose themselves to such dangers? The flesh of the one-horned ass was too bitter-tasting to be eaten with enjoyment. But there were other parts of the sought-after beast which served human needs. One of the fetlock bones, the quite heavy, cinnamon-colored ankle bone, was popular for use as dice. We know Romans played with cubes made from the bone, known in modern anatomy as the talus, though as far as they were concerned, it did not come from the unicorn but from the cow. The hunters' prize was, however, the horn, which could be made into a magical drinking vessel. According to ancient and oft-repeated reports, a draft from such a beaker warded off cramps, epilepsy, and a gamut of other diseases. Most important among its powers was that of neutralizing poison and protecting one using the vessel from any contaminated drink. Obviously such a prophylactic was in great demand at the courts of Asian rulers. Centuries later, Charles the Bold of Burgundy and other spiritual and secular princes of the Renaissance were still demanding a fragment of unicorn and a unicorn place setting to be always present on their dining tables.

Perhaps the Greek historian whose writings introduced the unicorn to European knowledge saw a unicorn goblet in use at the Persian court he attended, although he never exactly asserted he saw the beast or even visited its habitat in India. Ctesias of Cnidas was, like his father and grandfather, a physician by profession, as was fitting for such a family—his pedigree could be traced back to Aesculapius, the god of medicine. Ctesias himself spent eight years as physician-in-ordinary to Artaxerxes II (Mnemon), king of Persia, whose reign began about 405 B.C. When that monarch was wounded in 401 B.C. at the battle of Cunaxa by a spear hurled by his brother Cyrus, it was Ctesias who dressed his wounds.

This Greek evidently conducted himself with aplomb in the conniving company of courtiers and in 398 B.C. returned to Greece a wealthy man. He returned not to his native island but to the Peloponnesus, where he began writing his *Persica*, a history of Assyria and Babylonia. There he set down his own experiences and the things he had learned from other sources, including stories of India and the Far East told by merchants and envoys to the Persian court, and the result enjoyed wide readership over a long period. Alexander the Great is said to have devoured those reports on the mysterious East—and that of course had consequences more far-reaching than is the usual case when young people start reading of alien worlds.

Alexander's tutor Aristotle was obviously sceptical of Ctesias's writings and quoted them with perceptible reservation in his own book on animals. Although Ctesias maintained that he would not report anything he had not seen for himself or learned from trustworthy sources (and that he had indeed omitted several well-vouched items in order to avoid any suspicion of implausibility), he does not enjoy any particular reputation for reliability in the world of learning. Labelled as conceited, mendacious, and too indolent for serious studies, he has nevertheless been cited frequently with or without acknowledgment. For centuries natural scientists, physicians, and artists based their work on his commentary on the unicorn.

What was the foundation of Ctesias's information? It is easier to determine what did *not* contribute to his picture of a one-horned ass. For one thing, although hunting the wild ass was one of the favored diversions of Near Eastern monarchs, as confirmed by spirited Assyrian friezes, those asses had neither single nor multiple horns. Was a unicorn suggested by depictions seen on travels with the king? Certainly Ctesias had seen pictures in Persepolis and possibly also in the by-then ruined stones of Nineveh and on the walls of Babylon. Modern excavations have made accessible once more the Ishtar (Earth Mother) Gate from Babylon. Visiting the Islamic Department of the Bode Museum in East Berlin, one can see one-horned beasts advancing in solemn procession down a street towards the gate. Also revealed is a remarkable dragon-faced hybrid with erect horn. But these animals can scarcely have been the prototypes for Ctesias's description, despite occasional suggestions to that effect. Those one-horned beasts do not look like asses but more like bulls, and the head of that hybrid has been identified as an enormously enlarged head of a viper (with two horns). Furthermore, the bull-like beasts may well possess two horns, seen in profile as one. If we join the scholars who insist they are one-horned, we might venture too far afield. If we take these as unicorns, the number and form of the fabulous beast may exceed all bounds: countless reliefs and cylinder seals from the regions of India, contemporary Pakistan, various Near Eastern cultures, and Egypt provide us with a plethora of profiles of horned beasts.

A relief in silver on a huge sacrificial cauldron found in Denmark offers one of the innumerable unicorns in profile. The circular growth of hair around the horn seems to indicate we should interpret it as a unicorn. Of that we can't be sure, but it is an oriental beast. The cauldron was scuttled in a bog on the Jutland peninsula as a votive offering to the gods and was rediscovered near Gundestrup. It is not a product of the north, however. It must have been manufactured in the territory of the eastern Kelts in the Balkans or by the Black Sea, since battle depicted appears to stem from the world of Keltic myths and rites. Presumably it dates from the first century B.C. The work is now in the Danish National Museum, Copenhagen.

The one-horned bull attacked from behind by a lion, or the rampant leonine monster which a struggling king is gripping by its mane (or by the horn?) might have served Ctesias – and particularly later writers – as corroboration for the existence of single-horned beasts. Yet once again, these were not the primary foundation for the Grecian physician's report. His unicorn was of a different stripe. To conclude with what his unicorn was not, we should note that Ctesias's writings say nothing of such animals in the form of rams or bucks. That absence is interesting, for there do exist one-horned ibexes made in bronze long before his time. Such figures originating from the northern part of what we now call Iran are droll, aggressive miniature creatures about three inches tall. [Ill. 1]

One thing Ctesias expressly states is that India was the habitat of the curious animals. We know he never went there himself but must have heard, either face to face or second or third hand, from merchants, travelers, and probably drinking companions, a great deal about the wonderland of India. We must also suppose he added a few touches of personal imagination. If we read him carefully, we find he claims only to have seen one specimen for himself, that almost cubical bone from the fetlock joint, reddish-brown throughout yet similar to that of horned cattle. All in all, then, his account of the unicorn raises many fundamental questions and problems. Nevertheless, it had considerable influence.

About a hundred years after Ctesias's first presentation of what was assumed evidence, Megasthenes, a Greek of rank and authority who moved in royal circles and conversed with sages, did in fact visit India. He went there on a diplomatic mission for Seleucus I, who founded a large, though short-lived, empire in the Near East after the partition of Alexander's realm. Upon return, he wrote *Indika* in four books, the most complete account of India then known to the Greeks. Alexander's campaigns had greatly stirred their imaginations, and Megasthenes's more topical reports must have caused a sensation. His own personality gave them the seal of reliability, but unfortunately his dispatches have come down to us only as extracts in the writings of others and must be carefully reconstructed. Among items attributed to him is one account of a peculiar type of Indian unicorn called cartazoon in the local language. We can attribute to him the description but no personal observation whatsoever; once again the unicorn comes to us through recourse to still other authorities, in this case learned Brahmans.

Though again the size of a horse, maned, and dun-colored, Megasthenes's creature seems quite distinct from Ctesias's one-horned ass. Specific speed is not mentioned but the beast is credited with excellent hoofs which were, like the feet of the elephant, without distinct segments. Its tail was curly as a hog's. The horn grew between the eyebrows, not on the nose, and was black, extremely sharp, and impregnably strong. Megasthenes was the first to mention a detail which worked its way into classic representations of the unicorn: spirals on the horn. He was also the first to speak of the animal's exceedingly raucous bray, which finds its echo in many later accounts.

The characteristics of the feet and tail might be interpreted as relating to the rhinoceros. However, Megasthenes has a separate chapter devoted specifically to the rhinoceros, which is distinguished from the cartazoon by its conflicts with other species, notably with the elephant for grazing grounds. Brutal fights ended with the rhino disemboweling its antagonist (a feat later transferred to the unicorn). His unicorn kept to itself in the impassable mountains in the hinterland of India, where animals known to Europeans as domestic stock, namely dogs, goats, sheep, and cattle, roamed at large.

Though remarkably gentle towards other species of animals, the cartazoon was pugnacious towards its own kind, and battles to the death often ensued. Only in the rutting season was the beast mild with its mate, grazing quietly alongside her. As soon as consummation had taken place, he again became unsociable and wild. Nowhere in these accounts do we read that an adult beast was captured, although colts and fillies were frequently brought to the palace and displayed in festivals.

One can only speculate to what degree the love of solitude which Megasthenes ascribes to the cartazoon stemmed from the beliefs of his Brahman sources. This quality was probably an important element of Hindu cults long before the advent of Buddhism. It is reflected in the book by Bengt Berg, the Swedish writer on zoology, who relates how he went in search of (and of course found) *his* own unicorn in the Indian rhinoceros.

Ioan. Stradanus invent.   *Ioan. Collaert sculp.*   *Ioan. Galle excud.*

Non procul a ripis Asinos venatur agrestes   *In fronte : hinc phialæ fiunt et pocula, morbos*
29.   *Indus, permissu Regis : cornu quibus exstat*   *Quæ sanant, vulnus curant, pellunique venena .*

4. Unicorn hunt in India: Engraving by
   J. Collaert, after J. van der Straet
   (1523-1605) who drafted cartoons for
   Gobelin tapestries

There he quotes a "*Hymn of Buddha*" with end-verse refrain; the first stanza reads:

> *Like a lion, without fear of the howling pack,*
> *Like a gust of wind, ne'er trapped in a snare,*
> *Like a lotus blossom, ne'er sprinkled by water,*
> *Let me, like a unicorn, in solitude roam.*

15

The animal mentioned in the refrain is scientifically translated as rhinoceros. In the following chapter we shall see how the confused and confusing usage of unicorn and rhinoceros persisted through the Middle Ages. It is debatable whether any genuine hymns of Buddha are now known but the poem quoted by Bengt Berg *is* included in the sacred writings of Buddhism.

The mildness and need for solitude which the Brahmans described, whether factually of the rhinoceros or of the legendary cartazoon, has retained its religious significance. In the Buddha legend there is a gazelle which is on its knees in order to listen to the Master's original sermon in Benares. The horn between its ears is seen as a symbol of Nirvana. In the Rietberg Museum in Zurich there is a seventeenth-century Tibetan statuette of a unicorn on bended knees. It bears no resemblance to the rhinoceros but may have evolved from a mountain sheep. Like the gazelle it seems to be in quiet contemplation, and its expression of mildness could not be more profound. [Ill. 38]

Did the notion of a one-horned animal travel eastward from India in the same way that it came westward? Or, conversely, could China have been the original home of the unicorn? The first notice of the beast in China (where its horn is said to have been marketed as an aphrodisiac even down to this century) has been placed as far back as 2697 B.C. Extant descriptions of *chi-lin,* the Chinese unicorn, remind one of European conceptions of the animal: a body like an axis deer, horse's hoofs, an oxtail, as well as a horned, wolf-like head. King of the 360 animal species then recognized, *chi-lin* was reputed to reach 1000 years of age. We are told it could emit beams of the five sacred colors. Perhaps with equal fantasy it was thoroughly good-natured and possessed a musical voice. It kept to the beaten path, careful not to trample on living creatures and plants during its travels. The role of this marvelous beast was similar to that of the stork in Europe – to bring children (at any rate male babies) into the world. The birth of Confucius was but one of those announced by a *chi-lin*.

Chronologically midway between Ctesias and Megasthenes, our two chief classical sources regarding the antiquity of the unicorn, stands Aristotle, who exerted a tremendous influence on the medieval mind in both the occident and the Arabic worlds. Aristotle may have been reserved in his reliance on Ctesias and may not have accepted the idea of a unicorn goblet protecting the user from poison and disease, but he did believe in the unicorn's existence. He even produced a theory to fit the case. He explained how solipeds such as the ass were naturally fitted to be single-horned, more so than cloven-hoofed animals, since hoof and claw consist of the same substance as horn. That is, the solid hoofs of a soliped use more horny substance, leaving less for the horn itself, and so the ass tends to be only one-horned (when horned at all). Aristotle does, however, allow one exception. He has heard of another unicorn, the oryx, which, like other antelopes, was cloven-hooved but one-horned. Writers in later ages sided mostly with Megasthenes in assuming that the unicorn had a cloven hoof, though ascribing to it the form of a horse. When medieval scholastics in Germany (especially Albertus Magnus, probably the most influential scholar of the Middle Ages) resuscitated Aristotle's philosophy, they disseminated his theory on animals as well. [Ill. 3]

Inheritors of those ideas have, like Aristotle, turned to Africa and Arabia to seek the home of the unicorn, with the oryx antelope as its prototype. Several years ago an expedition left England for Arabia with the object of protecting the last specimens of the oryx from extinction. Its story is told by Anthony Shephard in *The Flight of the Unicorns*. Bengt Berg, who, strictly speaking, was seeking the unicorn in some other animal, photographed a black buck standing with its beautifully spirated horns in profile and he actually produced a lovely "unicorn" picture – a useful warning against those numerous oriental unicorn silhouettes.

But let us return to the journey of the unicorn from ancient Greece. Coming into the Roman world, we find Pliny has provided a third model of single-horned creatures: the Indian ox. His impassively scientific manner allows no digression into the miraculous and questions the prophylactic properties of the horn. The unicorn is also mentioned by Caesar, in the famous chapter of tall tales in his *Gallic War* where he speaks of the denizens of the Hyrcanian forest. He describes a deerlike ox; its single horn rises firmly midway between the ears and at the end it branches into the shape of a hand with several points. Caesar's unicorn is not, however, devoid of knee joints, as is occasionally asserted; that would apply rather to the elk, whose relationship to this image of the unicorn is hardly mistakable.

The real transmitter of Grecian unicorn lore to the world of imperial Rome and through that to Christian authors of the Middle Ages was Aelian, an Italian of the second century A.D. One of his chief works is *De animalium natura,* a collection of curious tales of animal life often illustrating a moral. He was a zealous compiler of excerpts, especially scientific writing, and bequeathed to later generations of philologists the tasks of discovering the sources of his learning and of reconstructing the works of earlier writers from the fragments they had left behind them. He was an industrious man, and although he never went outside Italy, he is said to have spoken Greek so excellently that he might have been taken for an Athenian. Certainly Aelian put the works of Ctesias to some use. And it was he who supplied us with that chapter attributed to Megasthenes making the unicorn suspiciously similar to the rhinoceros.

5. Dispute between four-footed and winged beasts: Woodcut from German illustrated edition of Aesop's Fables, *ca.* 1476

Yet in the course of half a millennium, views on the nature of the unicorn had been further increased without clear knowledge of the sources. According to Aelian, there are single-horned horses as well as asses in India, the horns of each being used for drinking vessels. The use of valuable unicorn goblets is reserved, he writes, for Hindus of the highest caste and "they decorate the horn with golden rings at intervals as though adorning the arms of a beautiful statue with ribbons." This custom continued into Renaissance Europe when gold and silver chased goblets of unicorn horn were still produced. In the seventeenth century the German poet Andreas Gryphius wrote a nuptial ode to some friends of his in which he was

still celebrating that night,
When almost engulfed in joy and rapture,
We supped the bouquet of noble wine from gold and unicorn.

Leaning on Ctesias, Aelian describes the asses more precisely than the horses and modifies some details; the horn now becomes a cubit and a half long and the fetlock bones are not cinnamon-colored but black throughout. As before, however, unicorns remain the fastest of all animals and to pursue them is to chase the unattainable. [Ills. 140, 143]

At least one later Roman, an itinerant miracle worker credited with a penchant for magic, saw the famous animal himself. This was Apollonius of Tyana, a disciple of the School of Pythagoras, who lived during the first century A.D. His biographer tells us that Apollonius also travelled to India where he encountered the gymnosophists, or naked philosophers whom we call fakirs, and saw the unicorn in the alluvial region of the Hyphasis (the river, now called the Beas, reached by Alexander on his march to India). He also heard of the qualities of the horn. When a student travelling in his company asked what might be thought of that, he replied, "I am inclined to believe it if they tell me that the king of these Hindus is immortal. For would one who can offer me or anyone else so healthy and therapeutic a draft, have any reason not to draw it for himself every day and drink from such a horn to the verge of intoxication?" That sounds less like a sorcerer than an intellectual.

Neither Greeks nor Romans have left any pictorial record of the unicorn. Either through oriental influences or their own imagination, they did give form to all sorts of unfamiliar or improbable things in nature – centaurs, sphinxes, and ram-headed fauns – but it is fruitless to look for the unicorn on vases in their temple friezes. It did not invade myth, fable, and fiction; it had no place in their cultural world but remained confined to the realm of scientific and geographic speculation. A unique freak such as the one-horned ram that, according to Plutarch, was born on the estate of Pericles was simply a welcome object for priests and soothsayers. As one German professor states somewhat austerely, "In the truly classical period the unicorn plays a wholly subordinate part, for at a creditable level of erudition, its aura had to disappear like ghosts vanishing at the coming of daylight. The heyday for this curious figment of the imagination was the eclipse of medieval scholasticism." That indeed is true. It must be said that despite an unbroken tradition, the medieval unicorn was really something quite distinct from the beast it had been in antiquity. One almost hesitates to use the same term for the two creatures.

3. The Biblical Beast

*God brought them out of Egypt; he hath as it were the strength of a
unicorn.*   Numbers 23:22

*His glory is like the firstling of his bullock, and his horns are like the
horns of unicorns; with them he shall push the people together to the ends
of the earth.*   Deuteronomy 33:17

*Will the unicorn be willing to serve thee, or abide by thy crib? Canst
thou bind the unicorn with his hand in the furrow? or will he harrow
the valleys after them? Wilt thou trust him, because his strength is
great? or wilt thou have thy labor to him? Wilt thou believe him, that
he will bring home thy seed, and gather it into thy barn?*
                                                        Job 39:9-12

*Save me from the lion's mouth; for thou hast heard me from the horns
of the unicorns.*   Psalm 22 (21):22*

*The voice of the Lord breaketh the cedars; yea, the Lord breaketh the
cedars of Lebanon. He maketh them also to skip like a calf; Lebanon
and Sirion like a young unicorn.*   Psalm 29 (28):5-6

But my horn shalt thou exalt like the horn of a unicorn.
                                                    Psalm 92 (91):11

*The sword of the Lord is filled with blood, it is made fat with fatness,
and with the blood of lambs and goats, with the fat of the kidneys of
rams; for the Lord hath a sacrifice in Bozrah, and a great slaughter in
the land of Idumea. And the unicorns shall come down with them, and
the bullocks with the bulls.*   Isaiah 34:6-7

If you turn to some of the modern translations of the Bible in search of
unicorns, you will be disappointed. There is no mention at all of them, only
of wild oxen or buffalo. Yet, as we see from the quotations at hand, one
translation flatly calls the unicorn a unicorn. It was the Bible prepared by
Martin Luther, who of course lived in an age familiar with the idea of the
beast.

* Figures in parentheses indicate Vulgate numbering of the Psalms.

20

Luther's work was influenced also by the Vulgate and earlier Septuagint versions of the scriptures. The latter was commissioned in the third century B.C. by Ptolemy II of Egypt (285–242 B.C.). A Macedonian by birth, he sent seventy-two learned Jews onto the island of Pharos near Alexandria to produce a Greek translation of the Old Testament within seventy-two days. Their translation of the Hebrew word *re'em* was monoceros, that is to say, unicorn. Many modern versions prefer "wild ox" (aurochs), which is now said to be the correct meaning of the term, but the men of the Septuagint did not know that animal, which by their time was extinct in the Near East. Perhaps the cattle those ancient sages did know seemed inadequate to express the idea of the strength and majesty commanded by this particular creature. We can't tell where they got their idea of the unicorn: possibly from the Greek writers or from Indian accounts which might have reached Egypt by the caravan routes. Perhaps they knew the African (not truly single-horned) rhinoceros. Whatever the circumstances, these men led the unicorn into the Bible.

The Septuagint term was adopted by the standard Latin version of the Bible in the Roman Catholic Church, the Vulgate, and that is how the unicorn got into the Palm Sunday mass. The Vulgate rests on the labors of St. Jerome, who reportedly began work in A.D. 383 and carried on during time spent as a recluse in Syria. He might have learned something of Asiatic concepts of the unicorn during that sojourn, but he could not have had a particularly clear picture of the beast in his mind's eye. He used the Greek terms monoceros and rhinoceros indiscriminately alongside the Latin *unicornis*. That remained a practice for centuries. Even in the late Middle Ages, we can see illustrations of an equine creature with a tapering horn on its forehead labelled rhinoceros.

Only once in its original tongue does the Old Testament mention an animal with one horn. The prophet Daniel speaks of the vision in which he saw himself conveyed to the palace at Susa. There he saw a ram with two tall horns, one taller than the other. "No beasts might stand before him . . . he did according to his will and became great." Then a he-goat came from the west with a "notable horn between his eyes." He bore the ram to the ground and smashed his two horns. Now the he-goat waxed very great "and when he was at his strongest, the great horn became broken." In its place four majestic horns sprouted. Daniel heard a voice interpreting this apparition as indicating the destruction of the kingdoms of Media and Persia by the "king of Grecia," obviously Alexander; Alexander the Great is represented by the first single horn of the mighty he-goat, the four horns growing in its place stand for his successors, the Diadochi. That is, of course, a hindsight prophecy. It is found in the eighth chapter of a book which was written long after the events "foreseen" in it had indeed occurred. [Ill. 19]

This sole "genuine" Biblical unicorn has seldom been depicted. At the end of the tenth century, Spanish monks produced impressive illustrations for a commentary on the book of Daniel ascribed to St. Jerome. You can see the prophet in the palace at Susa, the arrogantly strutting ram with its two distinct horns which are broken off by the he-goat, who carries not only his mighty single horn but also the four small ones which are already visible. Moorish influence is quite evident in the adornment of these miniatures; the East has had an effect on their content and their form.

The unicorn maintained a place in the Church and thus in art through the monoceros of the Septuagint translation. Because this text or its Vulgate version were the sources available to the Fathers of the Church when they began their Bible commentaries, the unicorn became incorporated into early medieval theology. Classical accounts, particularly the versions of Aelian and Pliny, may have become interwoven into the patristic writings. In the main, however, the Church Fathers appear to have nurtured an independent branch of unicorn lore. However many times the beast appears in the scripts of the Fathers (and even the most assiduous reviewers of their works can cite only a few quotations), they stick to St. Jerome's vague notions of the phenomenon. Their contributions to unicorn tradition were not universally accepted. For example, they frequently describe the horn as set on the nose, but people in antiquity and the Middle Ages had so rarely seen a real rhinoceros that it could not permanently affect the unicorn image.

From what we can read, none of the Fathers of the Church saw a unicorn. But apparently in the sixth century one of them did come very close to doing so. He lived in Alexandria during the reign of Justinian and his name has come down to us as Cosmas. A merchant, he made lengthy trips across the Red Sea to Arabia, East Africa, and even as far as India; on that account, his fellow countrymen are reported to have given him the nickname of "Indian Sailor." His latter days were spent in a priory in Sinai, where he wrote a conscientious account of the experience and knowledge he had gained during his lifetime. Conservatively he defended the old and established concepts of the universe and incorporated them into the composition of his *Topographia christiana* to oppose such newfangled ideas as the Ptolemaic system or that absurd conception that the earth might be spherical in shape. In relating his own experiences he wrote he had seen statues of unicorns in the four-towered palace of the ruler of Ethiopia, in a region where even during the nineteenth century some European scholars were investigating reports of the beast. Through Cosmas one particular trait of the unicorn's defiant character has been recorded for our delectation. Cosmas was informed that when a unicorn is surrounded by hunters and no other recourse is left, it somersaults into the nearest abyss, breaking the fall with its horn, and thus making good its escape.

We have no pictorial representations of the unicorn from the first centuries of Christendom, just as we have none from antiquity, but it was repeatedly used in symbolism in the East and the West. The beast could stand for both good and evil. Principally it is an image of irrestrainable strength. Man – take Job for example – is unable to tame it. This was a favorite motif when the unicorn began, about the ninth century, to appear in illustrated manuscripts of the Book of Psalms and the Gospels. We saw earlier that in Psalm 22, the first words of which supplied the cry from the cross, there is a plea

6. The unicorn in paradise, from Johann Joachim Becher's *Parnasus Illustratus Medicinalis,* (Ulm, 1663)

for rescue from the horns of unicorns. In the thirty-fourth chapter of Isaiah unicorns appear as one symbol for the heathens which the prophet is threatening in so formidable a manner. The unicorn was identified by the Church Fathers with everything resisting the domination of Christ and contrary to the Church. In Psalm 37, Jerome speaks of enemies of the Lord who are as overweening as unicorns, although this interpolation does not appear in the original text. Jews also, with their more austere monotheism, were symbolized by the *one* horn. Ecclesiastical antisemitism, which has banefully travelled down the ages, is revealed here too, perhaps more subtly than elsewhere. Finally, the Devil himself is represented as a unicorn in patristic works and Coptic incantations. [Ills. 13, 17]

Pope Gregory the Great called the Prince of Darkness a unicorn (and likewise the domineering princes "the mighty ones of our generation"). Gregory rediscovered the contradiction of the unicorn's power for good and for evil in a historical character. In a lengthy theological treatise, he compared Saul of Tarsus to a unicorn when he frenziedly persecuted Christians. But God succeeded in tethering this unicorn to the manger, fed it the fodder of the holy script, and harnessed it to his plough. Thus Saul became converted into Paul – God placed his trust in that unicorn.

The unicorn had become a positive symbol long before Gregory. The high spirits and strength of the young unicorn in Psalm 29(28), poetically extolled in the Vulgate as a "son of unicorns," referred to Christ. *Christus spiritualis unicornis* is an etherealized formula not of coarse identification but of symbolic treatment begun by early Fathers of the Church. St. Ambrose, bishop of Milan in the fourth century, inquired, "Who then has one horn, unless it be the only-begotten son, the unique word of God, which has been next to God from the very beginning?" Standing apart from the beliefs of his time, he raised serious doubts about the unicorn, for indeed "the unicorn itself, so experts say, is not to be found among generations of beasts." Even after a millennium and a half he has still been classified as an "enemy of the unicorn." But his doubt actually led him to a spiritual interpretation; the growth of the horn indicated a process of attaining full growth and maturity. "If therefore horns grow in some sense out of the head of our soul, then they apparently denote a process of perfecting the virtues." Ambrose exploits the phonal similarity between unicorn and unigenital, so that the horn later came to imply the unique might and the unique realm with which Christ is endowed. Augustine and others perceived in the single horn a symbol for the unity of the faith, and all those who adhered to this unique faith were called unicorns on that account but at the same time the enemies of that faith were similarly identified: quite early the horn had also been compared to the cross or to its upright.

8. Wild Man killing unicorn on damsel's
lap: Franconian woven tapestry,
ca. 1450. Hunter, with lover's knot
round his head, embodies lust in this
secular depiction

9. Miniature from *Physiologus* manuscript, *ca.* twelfth century. Unicorn description based on Megasthenes and/or Aelian

10. Eleven-century tapestry of creation,
◁ Gerona Cathedral, Spain. Adam is
naming the animals in right central
section

11/12. Virgin and unicorn in two
Byzantine manuscripts, ninth century.
Khludov psalter (right) and
Pantocrator psalter (below)

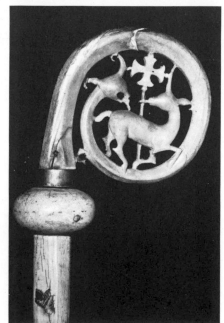

13. From the Averbode Book of the
    Four Gospels, twelfth century, the
    opening miniature to St. Matthew

14. Possibly the earliest Christian unicorn:
    fragment of relief on choirstall, sixth
    or seventh century Roman

15. So-called abbot's crosier of St.
◁   Boniface, Fulda, Germany, *ca.*
    thirteenth century

16. Pillar with mythical beasts from
    Souvigny Abbey, France, twelfth
    century. Horn of unicorn (between
    griffin and elephant) is broken off

17. Miniature for Psalm 22 (21) in
◁ Stuttgart psalter, France, early ninth
century

18. Eleventh-century font at present in
Freudenstadt Church,
Baden-Württemberg, Bavaria

19. Daniel's vision from a Spanish
miniature completed 970

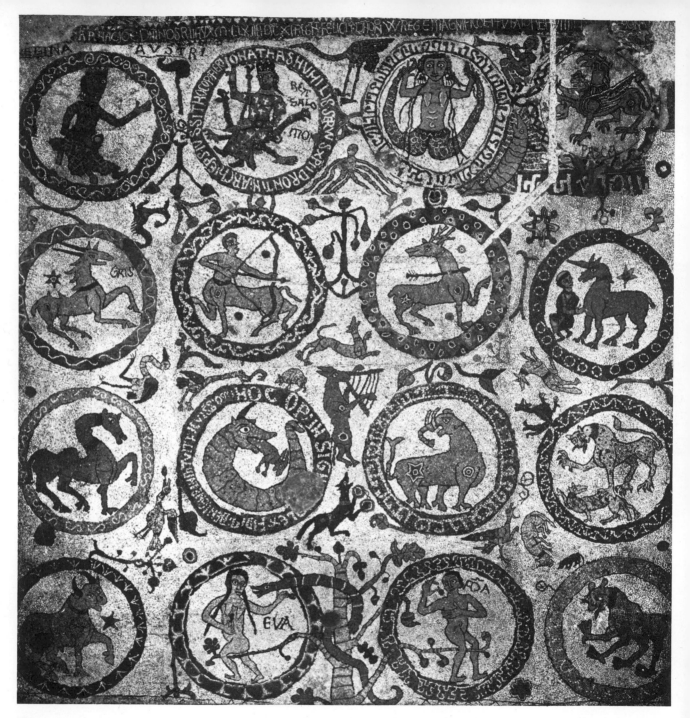

21. Portion of mythological
    bestiary in mosaic floor of
    Otranto Cathedral,
    Italy, twelfth century. Monk shown
    with unicorn possibly the artisan,
    Friar Pantaleone

35

22. Detail of Arabian ivory casket,
◁ *ca*. A.D. 1000

23. Dedicatory stone, *ca*. 1100, of former
▷ Holzkirchen (Germany) Abbey Church

24. Twelfth-century relief originally from
French abbey

37

25. Altar frontal with sacred beasts,
ca. A.D. 1300, now in Thun Castle,
Switzerland

26. Fourteenth-century chest front from
Westphalian region of Germany

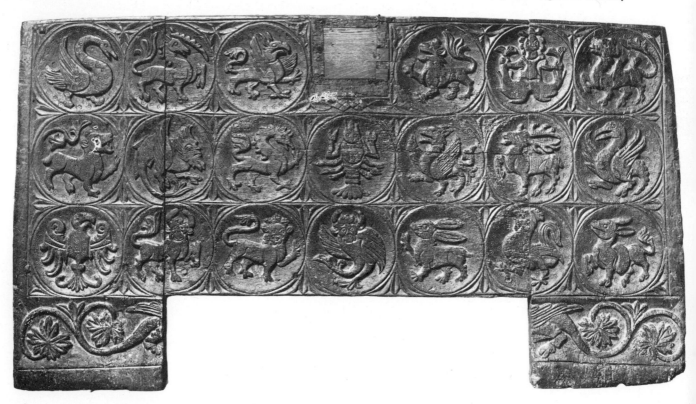

27. Detail of the "Malterer" Tapestry, 1310-20. The virgin taming the unicorn is part of a long fabric depicting various feminine wiles

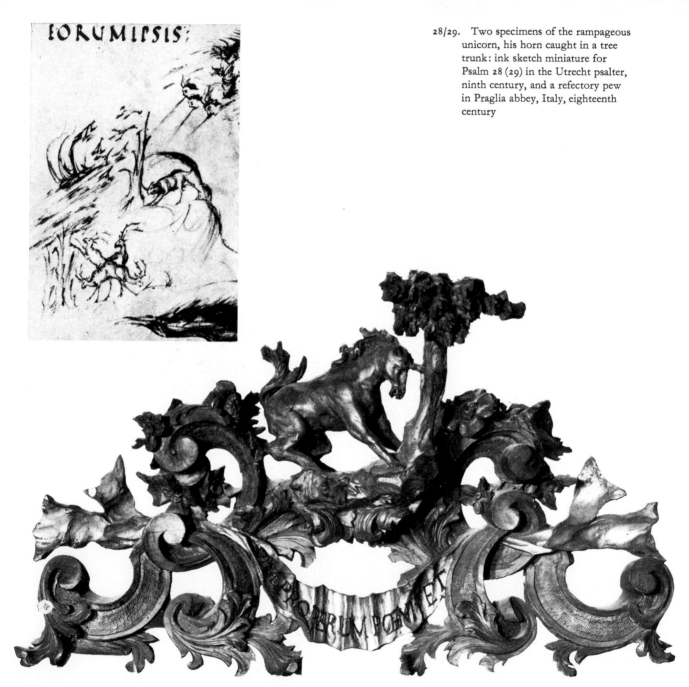

28/29. Two specimens of the rampageous unicorn, his horn caught in a tree trunk: ink sketch miniature for Psalm 28 (29) in the Utrecht psalter, ninth century, and a refectory pew in Praglia abbey, Italy, eighteenth century

Both the unicorn and the lamb of God are symbols of the Savior, stemming from comparisons made by early theologians. The venerable evidence showing that this parallel was accepted by subsequent periods includes the crosier shown in illustration 15. Although worshipped in the sacristy of Fulda cathedral as the abbot's staff of St. Boniface (according, by the way, to a not particularly ancient legend), that crosier cannot have been used by the Apostle of Germany. In his day, the eighth century A.D., such accessories were unusual, in Germany at any rate, and this item comes from a substantially later period, probably from the eleventh or twelfth century. It was presumably made during the reign of the Hohenstaufen emperor Friedrich II, in Sicily, where the traditions of Oriental craftsmanship were carried on. Artisans there would naturally have been prepared to fulfill the demands of Christian customers. The crook of the ivory crosier curves back into a viper biting the already collapsing unicorn. This portrayal of sacrificial death became one of the proofs of Christianity in Germany, where the faith was still incipient. Although in this case the silhouette may leave some ultimate shadow of doubt as to whether the assumed unicorn is not in fact a gazelle, its similarity in motif to the paschal lamb does admit christological interpretation.

Fulda monastery appears certainly to have had some early connection with the unicorn, whether it actually embodied the Lord, or more abstractly, stood for monastic solitude and discipline. Holzkirchen cloister near Würzburg, subordinated to Fulda by Charlemagne, has bequeathed a stone relief with unicorn, most likely of earlier date than the Fulda abbot's staff. Already in the Carolingian period under Louis I the Pious, the unicorn appeared in Fulda monastery in its other meaning as a symbol for a tough, violent man like Saul of Tarsus. One of Boniface's earliest successors was Ratgar, a highly gifted architect whose proficiency in reconstruction of the church so deeply impressed the friars that they unanimously elected him their abbot. In so doing, however, they cut a rod for their own chastisement. In his mania for construction, the new abbot so bullied his monks that they had hardly any time for prayer, much less leisure for meditation, and they therefore labelled him a "rampageous unicorn." He was portrayed as such in the chronicles of the abbey: he is shown standing, crosier in hand, in the narthex of his church – on the right half of the picture, however, the savage unicorn is smashing his way through the timorous, sheeplike flock of monks. The original miniature has been lost, but there is a replica in early seventeenth-century style which brings the incident and the symbol vividly to life. In the end, Ratgar was discharged by Emperor Louis at the persistent urging of the exasperated monks. [Ill. 31]

30. The unicorn refusing to board Noah's ark: woodcut by Tobias Stimmer (Basel, 1576)

At this time, Byzantine and Carolingian psalters displayed miniatures of the unicorn that, even though not the earliest, were certainly extremely early Christian representations. The seventy wise men who in the course of translation had created a beast have influenced biblical illustration down the ages. Although not expressly mentioned (even in the translated version of the Bible) as being present at the creation of the world, the unicorn belongs in that setting, to paradise, and to the readily illustrated naming of the beasts by Adam. It dominates others on the *Tapiz de la Creazión* ("Tapestry of the Creation") which dates back probably to the early eleventh century and now reposes in the treasury of Gerona cathedral in Spain. On a Flemish tapestry in the Academy of Fine Arts in Florence, the unicorn stalks in golden brilliance, proud and aloof at the head of all other beasts, distinguished before them all by the fact that the Lord hovers above him. [Ill. 10]

In the West Berlin Museum of Arts and Crafts this beast is shown in particularly sumptuous form on a Swiss tapestry of paradise made around the turn of the fifteenth century. With powerful horn he rests between Adam and Eve more prominently than all the other beasts. The serpent is not to be seen, but it has completed its work; the parents of mankind are wearing their fig leaves and stand in shame. From the heavens, the voice of the Lord rings down. But while the judgment is being thus announced, the unicorn is already promising future salvation. [Ill. 57]

Now a problem arises. With the unicorn thus already in the Garden of Eden, why is it not found in the Biblical events that follow? The most obvious explanation was that he may have succumbed in the deluge. Occasionally, though, pictures of Noah's ark show the unicorn mounting that rescue craft along with the other creatures. A contrary view is offered by a woodcut by Tobias Stimmer in an illustrated Bible printed in 1576. A unicorn couple remain behind, turning away with their familiar arrogance. But the unicorn might simply have been too large and heavy for the ark: the Talmud tells us it could even have been confused with a mountain. This hypothesis was openly held up to ridicule by one of the most erudite sleuths, Thomas Bartholin, the Danish physician, in the text he published in 1645. But no other has developed to solve the riddle. Only legend offers an "explanation." [Ills. 10, 30]

However it was, the *re'em* returned to the Jewish cycle of myth after its metamorphosis into the unicorn. Probably that was how it found its way into eastern European nursery tales. In two different contexts, the unicorn preserves its intractable nature. A Polish story relates that "When Noah let a pair of each animal board the ark, he also admitted the unicorn. However when this one jostled all the other animals Noah unhesitatingly drove it forth into the flood." It gets similar treatment in a Ukrainian folk tale. "All the beasts obeyed Noah when he admitted them into the ark. All but the unicorn. Confident of his strength he boasted 'I shall swim!' For forty days and forty nights the rains poured down and the oceans boiled as in a pot and all the heights were flooded. The birds of the air clung onto the ark and when the ark pitched they were all engulfed. But the unicorn kept on swimming. When, however, the birds emerged again they perched on his horn and he went under – and that's why there are no more unicorns now!"

Yet of course the unicorn is still with us. Having made its entrance during the earliest centuries of Christianity, it stands right alongside the ecclesiastical symbolic beasts, namely the lion of St. Mark, the bull of St. Luke, the eagle of St. John, and next to the dove and directly beside the lamb, symbol of divine sacrifice.

RATGARII ABBATIS SCHEMA.

31. Copper engraving of Abbot Ratgar of Fulda as the "Rampageous Unicorn" (Antwerp, 1612, after a lost ninth-century miniature)

4. Tales from Physiologus

The phoenix sets itself aflame to rise from its ashes with new life;

The pelican stabs its very breast to quicken its brood with its own life's blood;

The hungering fox shams dead to lure birds too near its lair;

The turtledove and turtledove do live in harmony together. . . .

One may have little idea of the richness of the literature and art surrounding the unicorn, but mention of that creature usually brings to mind the story of its capture by a damsel. That narrative, statements such as those above, and description of the unicorn are bedfellows in the book we have cited as a primary natural history source: *Physiologus*. The title does sound scientific as does the writing, at least on the face of it. Actually it is a collection of stories based on marvelous peculiarities of various natural objects, real or imaginary. Early preachers relied on its information to explain scriptural passages, and it eventually enjoyed a circulation second only to that of the Bible. The number of texts and variants is almost incalculable. It was translated into the languages of the Near East, particularly Arabic, Coptic and Armenian. Through Latin it penetrated widely into European vernaculars, Italian, French, German and even old Norse, as well as the Slavic tongues and Georgian. It inspired later bestiaries, and thus incipient science, natural history, and geography became mingled with the reports of ancient authors. Symbolic and allegorical contents were extracted by theologians who, within abbeys and monasteries, were often the same men who were artists, miniaturists and sculptors looking for inspiration. What use is it to us today, though? Its importance is assured by its being that third avenue which brought the unicorn to Europe from the Near East. But before we place *Physiologus* alongside the other extant depictions or evidence of the unicorn, the nature of the unique documentation should be re-examined.

Physiologus is a slim volume, author unknown, and date and place of original publication conjectural. As far as one knows, the original was a Greek manuscript; there may have been a still older version in an oriental

32. Seizure of the unicorn, from the ninth-century Bern *Physiologus*

language but this cannot be proven. The stories themselves may have been derived from popular fables, and some Indian influence is clear, as in the introduction of the elephant and the paradisiacal tree, and the unicorn. The character "The Natural Philosopher" appears in the book, but it is impossible to determine if the original author was using the third person to refer to himself or some other man of science. A few commentators thought Aristotle was probably this fictionalized author; a later version expressly names Solomon.

Long and arduous research has not satisfactorily resolved the problem of authorship – or even place of origin. For a time it was assumed that *Physiologus* had been written by a Christian in Alexandria in the first half of the second century A.D. (It was cited by writers subsequent to that period.) Alexandria was a traditional center of learning from antiquity to the Christian era and also a focus of trade where communications with the Near East and India could facilitate the passage of influence from those regions. But meticulous re-evaluation of source material aroused doubt. Indeed, some critics have vehemently asserted that the place of origin could only have been some Syrian city, most probably Caesarea, the time, the end of the fourth century A.D., and the original version, possibly Hebrew. Nevertheless, the balance of opinion now seems rather to veer once more to the earlier date and Egypt.

No extant manuscript is completely acceptable as the original *Physiologus* although there are numerous copies from various periods. Likewise, we have only copies of works by authors who are supposed to have used *Physiologus* as a source. And just think how easily a monkish copyist could now and again surreptitiously interpolate some idea of his own. One can gather some idea of the infinite labor such philological study demands from the *Recensions of the Greek Physiologus* edited by Francesco Sbordone, the Italian who disentangled underlying original texts from seventy-seven Greek manuscripts of which twenty-one alone had been preserved in monasteries on Mount Athos. He produced three editions which must, independently from each other, have had their source in some common original: (1) the earliest, containing forty-eight chapters, which came into existence presumably in the second century A.D.; (2) a Byzantine version of twenty-seven chapters which appeared in the fifth or sixth century; and (3) a version of thirty chapters from the tenth or eleventh century. This last had been ascribed erroneously to St. Basil, a great figure of the Eastern Church, who was archbishop of Caesarea in the fourth century. Sbordone further compiled in two parts a total of thirty-nine chapters which could not be fitted into any of the foregoing editions, and, finally, yet another rendering, in verse.

Varying in number of sections and content according to the different versions that have survived, the text contains a few dozen sections each dealing with one creature, plant, or mineral linked individually to a Biblical text. In reality, the scientific matter is merely a vehicle for the Christian theological and ethical commentaries which are the essence of the work. It speaks of the birth of dead lion cubs that come to life three days later at their sire's breath or roar – a symbol of the Resurrection. The fox's trickery of the birds (according to *Physiologus*) represents Satan the wily. Such stories may quite appropriately have embellished popular sermons in the period when the text came into existence. It cannot, however, be considered a theological text; it is too unsophisticated for that. It frequently reveals the poetic ingenuousness of fable.

The various compilations overlap abundantly in subject matter and frequently also in wording, although there are some noteworthy deviations as well. This is the case with the unicorn. Let us use the oldest rendition produced by Sbordone. Its twenty-second chapter is typical of the structure and narrative style of *Physiologus*. First, the Biblical quotation: "The Psalmist sayeth: My horn shall be exalted like a unicorn's." Next, the "scientific data": The unicorn is described as a small beast like a young he-goat and exceedingly mettlesome. Huntsmen cannot approach him because he is so strong. A single horn stands midway on his head. How can he be caught? A damsel is brought into the vicinity, and the unicorn leaps into her lap. The damsel quiets him and takes him along to the palace and into the king's presence. Finally, there is the practical Christian application: "The beast is transformed into the image of our Savior 'and has erected a horn of salvation in the house of his servant David,' and the horn of salvation grew toward us. The angels and the (heavenly) host could not constrain him, but he entered the body of the truly eternal virgin Mary, 'and the word became flesh and lived among us.' " No mention is made of the unicorn *as* the Christ child, but gospel and psalter manuscripts of the ninth century do show the Virgin with the unicorn alongside Old Testament citations. The Pantocrator psalter from Mount Athos even shows the Virgin Mary suckling her unicorn child. [Ills. 2, 12, 27, 32, 34]

The actual content of *Physiologus,* the shape and theme of its stories, may provide a more reliable clue to its origins and authorship than do the efforts of the philologists. For one thing, what *Physiologus* has to say about the unicorn is definitely not derived from Greek or Roman sources; this natural scientist did not, as has been sometimes assumed, collect the classical legends and convert them into Christian parables, at least not where the unicorn was concerned. The volume does not, as the Greek writings we have examined did, refer to either horse or ass or gazelle, and the elephant's feet which Megasthenes describes are nowhere to be found in the physiologist's account of the unicorn. *Physiologus* does, however, contain a small, literally capricious beast similar to those bronze statuettes from ancient Iran; this is pictured as cloven-hoofed like the oryx unicorn of Aristotle, and so it remained even when once more it achieved the stature of a horse in the Western world. Furthermore, the profoundly effective and durable legend of the capture of the unicorn by the Virgin and its religious implication did not come to us by way of the classics, for Greeks and Romans knew nothing about it. Alexandria is increasingly deemed to be where *Physiologus* was written, for there was an Indian community living there and such a story could well have come into hellenistic Egypt through the merchants among them.

Listen to the following fable: Once upon a time, in ancient and faraway India, a virtuous hermit lived in the forest with only the animals for company. A gazelle was wonderstruck at the sight of his well-favored body and thereafter gave birth to an offspring which had the figure of a man – with a horn growing from the middle of his forehead. For that reason he was called Unicorn. He too became a hermit.

A wicked monarch ruled the land, and for his sins the gods send down a severe drought. Brahman sages advised the king to have Unicorn brought to court, for this would end the punishing drought. So the king sent his beautiful daughter to the hermit whom she approached ostensibly as a repentant disciple. She succeeded in enticing the inexperienced ascetic to rapture and love, lured him onto a raft, and led him to the Court. Everything had a fairy-tale ending; the rains poured down, and the handsome holy man married the princess. (In some variants it is not the king's daughter but some other lady of the court who undertakes the seduction of the anchorite, but in all cases he certainly has to be taken to the king.)

This is without doubt the source of the *Physiologus* narrative. Trade communications between India and Egypt adequately explain how the legend may have reached the land on the Nile. Somewhere along the line of its journey this story became not one about a man called Unicorn but one of the fabulous beast unicorn. In this case, something was gained in translation. What an intriguing parallel between the effects of this error and the emergence of the unicorn in the Septuagint version of the Bible! Known thus through such dependable sources as Grecian writers and the Bible, the unicorn was easily accepted into early Christian literature and science. Realizing that the unicorn owes its existence to error need not detract from the charm of the story in which it is captured by a damsel. But it does illustrate the remarkable ways of the imagination which nurture an immaterial reality.

There are many versions of this fable. Japanese mythology also knows a single-horned demon in human form who is subdued and shackled by the

33. The water prodigy

hero Momotaro aided by some animals. In the eighteenth century a No play was produced about Ikkaky the sorcerer. He is depicted as living in Benares (India) and is the son of a doe. When he traps all the dragons and their ruler in a grotto, rain ceases to fall on the land. In this story, a beautiful lady of the court circle seduces the sorcerer, as commanded by the king, and robs him of his magical powers, thus liberating the dragons and allowing rain to pour down once more.

A number of versions predate the era of Buddhism and were incorporated into that literature. One scholar holds that Buddhism may have adopted the legend simply as evidence for its favorite theme of the baseness of woman; the story does appear in medieval Europe as an example of woman's wiliness, naturally with the unicorn as an animal. The story has even been made to come from the mouth of Buddha himself. He, after several transfigurations, resolved to devote his final earthly pilgrimage to the salvation of man and entered the womb of a woman to accomplish that. Thus he might have been embodied in the hermit Unicorn; the presence of the gazelle could have been included to explain the naming of the young hermit. Originally "Unicorn" may have had a purely symbolic significance, just as the rhinoceros, in fact, is adopted by Buddhism as a symbol for a quiet, powerful spirit inclined to solitude.

What was originally perhaps pure symbol became part of man's body of knowledge, a describable creature, which then gained an extraordinary, often, as we have suggested, contradictory range of symbolic value.

The allegory of the Savior's incarnation which appears in the most effective and widest spread story in *Physiologus* became an element of Christian mythology and scholastic theology for centuries. One phrase from that story has aroused much comment: the statement that "the heavenly host" could not restrain the Son made theologians speculate that the author of *Physiologus* might have been an adherent to Gnosticism. That religio-philosophical system, with which early Christianity waged a bitter battle, a struggle for survival, really, postulates a heavenly power between the Supreme Deity and the universe. Speculations about Gnostic authorship are relevant in deciding the date of *Physiologus*. If the book had been written later than the middle of the second century A.D., such Gnostic influences would necessarily have been more frequent and explicit. Until well into the nineteenth century, the question "Could the author of *Physiologus* have been a heretic?" was discussed by theologians and other scholars, occasionally with something approaching high passion.

Whoever the author, the symbolism is the important element in *Physiologus*. The capture of the unicorn by the virgin is by no means purely idyllic. If it is taken to be the incarnation of Christ, it is also the beginning of his calvary.

34. The unicorn subdued

It is not always the virgin who catches the unicorn, leading it gently to the king. Although it was her maidenly presence that lured and bemused the beast, brutal hunters prostrate the defenseless creature. Thus the event becomes a symbol of the earthly stations of the Master's cross. Religious allegory and terrestrial zest for pursuit lie intimately entwined and not always distinct from each other in artistic portrayals. [Ills. 7, 8, 43-50]

Physiologus was the inspiration for numerous medieval bestiaries where animal stories were distilled against a distinct background of Christian allegory. (Some unadulterated bestiaries have in their turn undergone many variations including references to plants and even stones.) In these the erotic character already innate in the Indian origins of the capture story is more accentuated. When the unicorn enters the Virgin's bosom, it takes the place of the Child that she will eventually bear; its horn is the definite symbol of virility subsiding into her body. The damsel lures the unicorn through her scent, shows him her knee and breast, actually taking him in as a lover or pet, and offers him her milk which so drugs the animal that it drops asleep in her lap. In other sequels, the unicorn transfixes the traitress with its horn when it realizes that this playmate is not truly a virgin.

The story of the maiden and the unicorn is the most fertile though not the only traditional unicorn tale emanating from *Physiologus*. One which supports the theory of Indian origins is the tale of friendship between the unicorn and the elephant. This elephant has no knee joint, and so he develops the habit of resting against a tree when going to sleep. Like the Germanic elk hunters mentioned by Caesar, hunters come and partially saw the tree so that the elephant, trumpeting loudly, tumbles to the ground with its lost support. Up rush the hunters from their blind, snatch the ivory from the jaws of the defenseless beast, and hastily make their escape to prevent "the unicorn catching up and making a hearty meal of them." If the unicorn does arrive in good time, it kneels beside its fallen comrade, tenderly works its horn beneath the pachyderm's body, and lifts him to his feet. Here, then, we have the Savior notion: "Our Lord Jesus Christ is denoted as a royal horn. When he sees man fallen and pitiable, our Lord of all Creation comes and sets him up again." The mastery with which the author of this story dismisses the question of contradictoriness of his allegories is noteworthy. The beasts themselves are not objects of comparison, only their qualities. "Animals have good and bad qualities. The good ones are compared to Christ and his saints, the bad to demons and wicked men." No equivocation there. The allegories are his concern, and they are based on the complexity of attributes within each creature [Ill. 39].

Here is another important tale, extracted from the fragments Sbordone gathered in making his *Physiologus* compilations: "There is a great lake in

49

those regions, where the animals congregate for drinking. However, before they assemble, the serpent approaches and spits her venom into the water. The animals detect the poison and dare not drink, but await the arrival of the unicorn. Up he comes, goes straight into the water and makes the sign of the cross with his horn, detoxicating the venom. The unicorn sips some of the water, and then all the other animals too can drink." The Greeks already knew of the purifying power of the horn from Indian sources. Now, however, the power depends on the living creature which is set so expressively in opposition to the serpent in her legitimate role, as it were, of foe of goodness and good people. That power actually becomes effective only through an act of sanctification. The absolving action of the sign of the cross links the unicorn yet again to Christianity. This scene is not commented on in *Physiologus*. The healing symbol is effective enough and combines with the older naturalistic notion of the antidotal potency of the unicorn goblet to contribute to the horn being highly honored as a medicine for hundreds of years. It added a glimmer of religious magic to the superstition of the ancients. [Ills. 33, 128]

Physiologus stands as a sort of funnel. Perhaps a loom would be a closer analogy. Its contents become part of the fabric of occidental tradition even as the volume collects strands of tradition which went before. In the version erroneously believed written by the Church Father St. Basil, accounts from the Septuagint and from antiquity are clear, only to further demonstrate the ambiguity of the unicorn allegory.

The so-called Basil version alludes to that psalm in which David prays for his rescue or, as is now customary to say, the salvation of his soul from the unicorns and continues: "The unicorn is evilly inclined toward man. It pursues him, and when it catches him up it pierces him with its horn and devours him." What a contrast that makes to the figure of the Redeemer! The author purported to be Basil in his commentaries pushes this contradiction to its full extent: "Take care then, O Man, to protect thyself from the unicorn, that is to say from the Devil. For he is ill-inclined toward man and skilled in doing him harm. For he stands by the way day and night and by permeating man with his sophistries severs him from God's commandments." Thus the same creature that denotes the Redeemer is also a symbol for his adversary. When the nineteenth-century German poet Friedrich Rückert wrote that a man was travelling in the land of the Syrians when a camel came by and chased him into the well, he is using a tale that travelled westward from India by way of Syria. In it the unicorn becomes a symbol of death, and this may well be the source for the so-called Basil manuscript and also the prototype for the unicorn with the crescent moon which foretold the fall of Byzantium.

Page from *Defensorium inviolatae virginitatis Mariae* (Compurgation of the Unsullied Virginity of Mary) showing other miracles of nature to "scientifically" establish the feasibility of Virgin Birth (see also "Commentaries on the Illustrations")

Si vinu̅ in fanguine̅ co̅uerfum fore claret. cur xp̅m veru̅ bomine̅ virgo no̅ generaret. iuftinus. i. libro. cap. iiij. ʒ valerius maximus.

Bonafa fi ore feta amare claret. cur angeli ex ore v̅go no̅ generaret. yfidorus. tij. etbimologiaʒ. ʒ gregori⁹ libro. xxx.

Si flumeu̅ in cruore tbolofe verfuʒ claret. cur v̅ga icffe flore virgo non generaret gilbertus in cronicis.

Rinoceron fi v̅gini fe inclinare valet. cur verbu̅ patris celici virgo no̅ generaret yfidorus ʒ alanus.

In the twelfth century a written oracle current in Byzantium concerned the imminent fall of the Comnenus dynasty. It was ascribed to Emperor Leo VI, the philosopher who reigned about A.D. 900. One such prophecy was accompanied by a sketch of a unicorn bearing aloft the emblem of Islamic peril, the crescent. Apparently two ideas are being synthesized here: treatment of the unicorn as a symbol of power among the early Church Fathers and its use as an image for Satan in the pseudo-Basilian version of *Physiologus*. The later *Physiologus* of the Waldenses (a twelfth-century Roman Catholic sect) identifies the unicorn with Satan, but the Basilian volume allows an alternative; as we have seen, the unicorn there is concurrently a symbol for Satan and for the Savior.

The death symbol is obvious in the following anecdote which interestingly enough also came from India originally:

> *Once there was a man, Barlaam by name, who lived in the desert near Senaah and who often preached against the illusory pleasure of the world. Thus he spoke of a man fleeing in haste from a unicorn who would devour him. Falling into an abyss or well he happened to catch hold of a bush but failed to find adequate foothold. With the raging unicorn glaring down on him from the rim of the well, he caught sight of a dreadful fiery dragon waiting with open maw for him to drop. From the narrow ledge on which he was teetering, four serpents distend their fangs. A pair of mice, one black and the other white, gnaw away at the roots of the bush to which he is still clinging, while the bush itself is about to break off. But as he lifts his eyes, he spots honey dripping from the branches of the bush and forgetting all about his peril he surrenders himself fully to the sweetness of the honey.*
>
> *The unicorn, as Barlaam expounded in his parable, was death which pursues man everywhere. The well was the world filled with every evil. The bush was human life eventually extinguished by the constant erosion of the hours of night and day represented by the black and white mice. The four serpents represented the human body composed of the four elements which must disintegrate if they become disturbed. The dragon is the bottomless pit of Hell threatening to swallow up mankind. But the honey is the worldly pleasure to which man surrenders forgetting all peril.*

Thus wrote Giacopo da Voragine (James of Viraggio), archbishop of Genoa, who in the thirteenth century published a selection of tales and anecdotes, entitled *Legenda aurea* ("The Golden Legend"). He elucidates the parable of Man who, encompassed by death in the midst of life, forgets all concern about his eternal salvation – a story which was also frequently retold and illustrated elsewhere in the Middle Ages. [Ill. 59]

37. Painted Romanesque beam (detail).
Barcelona, fourteenth or fifteenth
century

38. Seventeenth-century Tibetan unicorn;
the horn between the ears is
symbolic of Nirvana.

39. Elephant luring unicorn, Persian wall tile of probable thirteenth-century dating

40. Shadhahvar, the musical horn, appears on a fourteenth-century Arabian miniature

فيها فيخرج منه صوت في غاية الطيب ويجتمع الحيوانات حوله لسماع ذلك الصوت ٭ وقد ذكروا ان

قرن هذا الحيوان اهدى الى بعض الملوك فتركه عند هبوب الريح بيده ٭ فكان يخرج منه صوت خزين حتى
كاد من سماعه يجلب على سامعه البكاء ٭ ثم وضعوه معكوسًا فكان يخرج منه صوت حسن حتى كاد يدهش

41. Alexander the Great fighting the
    Carcadann. Persian miniature, early
    fourteenth century

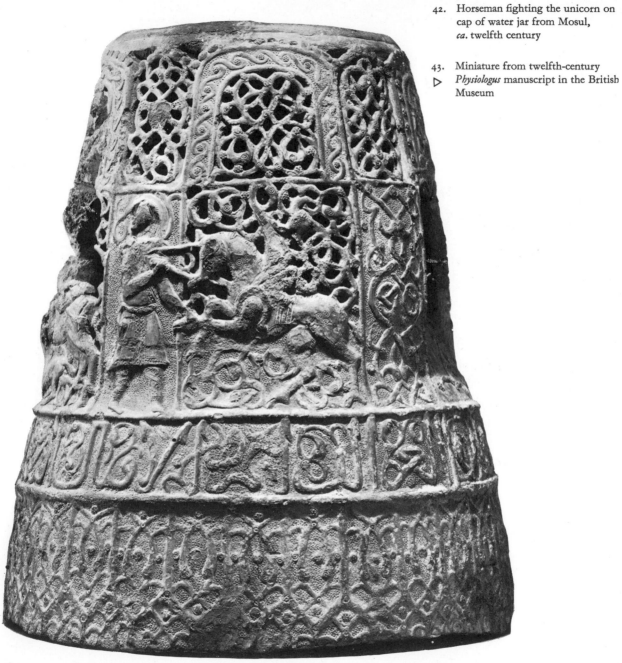

42. Horseman fighting the unicorn on cap of water jar from Mosul, *ca*. twelfth century

43. Miniature from twelfth-century *Physiologus* manuscript in the British Museum

Death of the Unicorn

44. Detail from a French fourteenth-century box

45. Detail on an Italian miniature, *ca*. fourteenth century

46. Detail on three-inch wide enamelled
silver salver, fourteenth century

48. From Stratford-on-Avon

Sacrifice of the Unicorn

47. Detail on choirstall, Cologne
◁ cathedral, early fourteenth century

Two Pieces by Pisanello

49. Medal combines chastity symbols to
▷ honor Cecilia Gonzaga of the
    reigning Mantuan family

50. Sketch: Innocence protects the
▽ unicorn

Few Dare Fight a Unicorn Without the Virgin Decoy

51. Detail from frieze in Strassburg
▽ Minster

52. Wild Man fighting unicorn on an
▷ early fifteenth-century woven
tapestry from Strassburg

The Unicorn

53. Detail on wall bracket in St. Vitus Cathedral, Prague, fourteenth century

54. Thirteen-century floor mosaic from
◁ the Chruch of S. Giovanni Evangelista (St. John the Evangelist), Ravenna, Italy

55. North portal of Altotting Collegiate Church, early sixteenth century

56. Annuniciation, as shown on
    mid-thirteenth-century altar frontal
    (antependium) at Goss, Austria. Detail
    includes the declaration "Abbess
    Cunigund made me."

57. Swiss Garden-of-Eden rug, *ca.* 1500, with unicorn signifying future redemption

68

Sharply contrasted, for example, would be a marble relief depiction from Ferrara cathedral, probably made shortly after Giacopo's masterpiece, and a picture by the Dutch engraver Bolsworth who gives it definite dramatic though unintentional baroque humor. The legend as such is still one of the finest parables for human existence. [Ill. 59]

The man may take refuge in a tree instead of a well. A thirteenth-century manuscript from Iraq which is now in the possession of the Bibliotheque Nationale in Paris shows this as in a filmstrip. The top line depicts the man still dining with friends, and below in three stages he is in flight onto the tree. The same scene appears in a mural painting in the church of the vineyard village of Bischoffingen (Germany). The man, magnificently garbed and carrying a falcon at his wrist, stands in a tree, the tree of life, while angels and demons contest for his soul, mice nibble at the root, and the unicorn charges at the trunk. Death, "Fear" too, ready to pluck the man like ripe fruit, carries a basket on his back similar to those the vintners take to the vintage.

The unicorn myth from the orient remained an exchange between East and West. It is not always clear which was the original stimulus. While the unicorn appeared in ninth-century Byzantine and Carolingian miniatures and occasionally in ivory insets, comparable Arabian reliefs are encountered only around the end of the first millennium, but there might have been earlier Arabian representations. In the eleventh and twelfth centuries when *Physiologus* was circulating throughout Europe in numerous translations and manuscripts, its effect is also traceable in the Moslem world. The unicorn appears in manuscript miniatures, in stances similar to those of the West, though also in other positions and forms. A twelfth-century earthen vessel shows a horseman slaying a charging unicorn. A slightly later Persian miniature shows the legendary hero Iskandar (none other than Alexander the Great – after more than a millennium and a half!) fighting a unicorn. The monster has a long tapering horn between its ears and huge wings on its shoulders. In another picture, a female figure is suckling a small graceful unicorn. At first glance this recalls the rare representation of the Virgin Mary in the Pantocrator psalter, but the text clearly deals with a scene of seduction. [Ills. 12, 41]

The myth of water purification by the unicorn did not merge into Moslem literature, although that element plays such an important part traditionally in the Orient. On the other hand, there is a slight echo of it in the cosmology of the Parsees, that sect which migrated to India in the eighth century from what is now called Iran and which still exists in its second homeland. Their Bundahish myth of the creation first came into existence in Pahlavi in the ninth century A.D. According to that legend, a three-legged ass, tall as a mountain, with six eyes and nine muzzles, stands in the midst of the ocean. It has a golden horn with openings from which a hundred smaller horns sprout varying in size from that of a camel, a horse, a bull, to an ass. With the horn it crushes all hostility of ill-intentioned animals. When it lowers its head into the ocean, it causes a great commotion in the waters, which then surge over the shores. When it calls out, all good female aquatic animals become pregnant and all the bad ones barren. When it urinates into the waters, they become purified, and if it does not make water, they all become tainted with the venom of Ahriman. In the dualist Zoroastrian religion, a one-horned ass stands beside Ormuzd and the powers of good.

As the unicorn concept rebounded from Europe to the Near East, other unicorn images were encountered that had emerged partly under Chinese influence since the days of Ctesias and Megasthenes. There was a whole gamut of single-horned beasts, not only large, strong ones but even hares. But these were apparently literary inventions more than anything else. The unicorn in action, in the mythical sense, was the Carcadann, large, strong and of ill temper, blessed also with magical powers – that was the beast with which Iskander (Alexander) fought. The figure, derived from a steer or buffalo, was frequently endowed with wings and possessed—or acquired—similarities to the occidental unicorn. It could be caught when lured into charging a tree or when entrapped by a maiden. It was strong enough to defeat an elephant. Its horn converted into goblets or ground to powder was therapeutic and strengthened sexual vigor. In addition, a belt made from the beast's hide was useful as a defense against disease—as with St. Hildegard of Bingen on the Rhine. Several features are clearly taken from occidental accounts; others found their way into Western lore probably through Africa and Spain. Yet altogether the Moslem unicorn seems to lack a certain quality. That seems to be the spiritual character which Christendom bestowed on its European avatar, on its embodiment of a model owing so much to the information provided by our National Philosopher. [Ills. 41, 58, 60]

5. Monstrous Symbols

What is the meaning of those absurd monstrosities, that astounding,
amorphous plethora of form, that formal opulence of shapelessness
standing in front of the eyes of studious monks in the cloisters? What
are those obscene apes doing there? Those savage lions? Those centaurs
and half-men? The striped tigers? And the fighting warriors? And the
horn-blowing huntsmen? There we can see many bodies with one head and,
conversely, many heads on a single body, here a quadruped with a serpent's
tail, over there a fish with a quadruped's tail. Over there a beast, horse
in front and goat behind, and again, a horned beast with a horse's rump.
Everywhere is such a rich and amazing profusion of different shapes, that
one would sooner learn from the statues than from books, sooner spend
the whole day doing that alone rather than contemplate the commandments
of God. By God, though people be not ashamed of these absurdities, why
at least do they not flinch at the expenditures?

Saint Bernard, founder and abbot of the twelfth-century monastery of
Clairvaux, was the iconoclast who thundered out this invective in an open
letter to Abbot William of Cluny. Bernard was a leader of the strict, puristic
reformed order set against the newly rich disciples of older reformers; he
was a man of intense and personal mysticism, opposed to external show,
crusading against waste of money on superfluous ostentation. [Ill. 16]

Nevertheless, he was astute enough to allow instructive images for
the benefit of lay people. Those monsters adorned the façades of Romanesque churches, crawled around the capitals of the pillars inside, and gazed
down from the timbered roofs. Three roads—antiquity, the Bible, and
Physiologus—had intertwined, bringing more than the unicorn into
the European experience. In the West, with its not overly mature, not too
deeply penetrated Christian tradition, where many a pagan lay barely
skindeep, they collided with relics of another world. This produced a
medley from which it was scarcely possible to unravel the original components, and in which concrete Christian tenets seemed in any case to be
thoroughly lost. The uncivilized images appeared only to interfere with the
desire of the flowering mysticism for direct communication of the soul with
God. And yet those images became a gateway to such an encounter.

That was a process which took centuries, and it had not yet fully matured in Bernard's day. Its probably started with Pope Gregory I (A.D. 590-604). The real initiator of the spread of papal power was a magnificent churchman though possibly not a great theologian. He came from a Roman patrician family, was well educated, and certainly not prone to superstition. In his discussion on Paul, for example, he used the unicorn purely as a symbol. **Presumably he did not favor making allegory too clear. But this pope, who** was prepared to travel through northern Europe in order to convert illiterates, may have sensed in allegory something of future value for preachment and clerical instruction. He did not consecrate a figure such as the unicorn, but he did legitimize it by using it in his writings. The precise details of such usage would be the concern of those who followed. He spread the story of the snaring of the unicorn by the maiden but did not link it to Christ.

That was the work of a somewhat younger contemporary, St. Isidore, Archbishop of Seville around A.D. 600. In particular, Isidore's *Etymologiae* is an encyclopedia of human and divine subjects, which transmitted an abundance of ancient beliefs and subject matter, both sacred and profane, to the Middle Ages. Isidore retold old stories of the unicorn's savagery, of its pride which drove it to death if captured, of its fighting the elephant, and even its entrapment by the maiden.

Medieval unicorn lore was fashioned from the writings of Gregory and Isidore. This continued up to the time of Albertus Magnus, who appeared **an expert naturalist in his bestiarium and maintained that tradition when** turning to mystic theology.

Only a small number of sculptural specimens from the early Middle Ages **survive, and these are partly open to question as to date and meaning. Apart** from miniatures in psalter and gospel manuscripts (dating somewhat later **than the eighth century) are the animal images which Bernard considered** scarcely pertinent to devotional studies. We can see some of these in churches and cloisters but their significance is not always clear: ancient traditions, pagan superstition, and curiosity about foreign lands allowed the content of Christian symbolism to penetrate only gradually. Motifs of the transitional period characteristically intermingle in the rug-pattern mosaic flooring in Otranto cathedral in southeastern Italy. That magnificent mosaic was begun in 1163, ten years after Bernard's death and was completed about three years **later. It depicts Adam and Eve, Noah, and other Old Testament characters** and includes Alexander the Great in his legendary attempt to hover in the air with the aid of griffins, a centaur, symbol of paganism, shooting the Christian stag, and also a unicorn and a monk – possibly Pantaleone, who is known to have been the creator of this carpet in stone. [Ills. 20, 21]

A contemporary of St. Bernard, Honorius of Autun (France), called the Great Unknown of the twelfth century, offered a literary example of the mixing of motifs. In *Speculum ecclesiae* he expounds the role of the maiden in trapping the unicorn as described previously in *Physiologus* and thus expanded the development of iconography. In his great geography *De imagine mundi* ("Picture of the World") on the other hand, he presents the unicorn in that wild irrational fauna said to inhabit distant India. This is a conglomeration of centuries of hunters', mariners', and soldiers' yarns, and it is doubtful whether any of it ever came direct from some truly Indian source. This wonderland is populated with humanoid animal hybrids and deformed people, but comparatively few pure animal figures. There are dog-headed humanoids with curling snouts covered with fur who howl like hounds; sciapods who, though one-legged, run faster than the wind and when they rest, they provide shade for themselves with their gigantic foot; other creatures without heads but with eyes in their shoulders and two holes in the chest instead of a nose and mouth; serpents so large that they eat a stag whole; ceucrocore, a creature with an ass's body, a stag's shanks, a lion's chest and forelegs, a gigantic cleft horn, pure gold teeth, and withal an almost human voice. Several beasts have pairs of mobile horns which they protrude and retract alternately for fighting purposes. The manticore has a human face, three rows of teeth, a lion's body, and a scorpion's tail; it eats human flesh and can take to flight in an emergency. Tortoises are so huge that spacious houses could be built from the shell. Compared with these monsters, which we see in many types of gargoyle, the elephant and the unicorn stand as rather harmonious and credible images. Honorius describes the unicorn essentially in the form reported by Megasthenes, that is to say with elephant's feet, a curly tail like a hog's, a long, tapering horn about forty-eight inches long, and a ghastly roar.

Some people have assumed that Honorius was outlining the basic concept for a pillar carved in relief of which, unfortunately, only the top portion remains at Souvigny in central France, once one of the foremost Cluniac priories. The various facets of this twelfth-century pillar show the duties for each month, a favorite motif in later prayer books, together with the zodiac, mythical characters, and monsters from Asia and Africa as described by Honorius. The pillar could scarcely have stood within the church but could reasonably have been a support for a sundial somewhere near the middle of the cloister, where the monks raising their eyes from their breviaries could see it as a manifestation of the world outside. On the pillar the unicorn stands midway between a griffin and an elephant, its damaged horn points backward, its ungainly feet are attached to slender legs, its tail is long and flourishes smartly with the coil like a hog's at its tip. [Ill. 16]

8. Cardunn from a thirteenth-century Iraki manuscript

73

Possibly the oldest and certainly the most impressive representation of the unicorn on German soil (dating to about 1100) appears on a baptismal font now in the seventeenth-century city church of Freudenstadt in the Black Forest. The sandstone material of the font indicates that it is of Black Forest origin, but nobody knows for which church it was originally intended. Its beautifully proportioned sandstone basin, with its pedestal forty inches tall, is supported by figures of wild beasts and humans. On the outside it bears symbolic patterns blending Christian and pagan motifs. Prominent among these is the unicorn, a powerful animal modeled somewhat on the lines of a rhinoceros, charging another animal resembling a lion. This has been interpreted as Satan roving around like a roaring lion seeking whom he may devour, while the unicorn symbolizes Christ fighting for the soul of the newborn. It is comforting to see Christ represented as a militant beast rather than the patient lamb, evidence indeed of the influence of the Eastern church which puts the King of Kings, Lord of the Universe, at the center of its creed in place of the Man of Sorrows. But this interpretation is open to question, and something more suitable for the atmosphere of childbirth and christening is derivable from the prayer in Psalm 22 (21) of the Stuttgart psalter: "Rescue me from the lion's mouth and protect me against the unicorns' horns." The unicorn seems rather to belong among the spellbound demoniac figures banished to the outside of the sanctuary. [Ills. 17, 18]

The other reliefs on the Freudenstadt font are difficult to interpret. Plainly visible behind the unicorn is a stag devouring (or spitting out?) a serpent. According to Pliny, the stag was among other things a serpent-killer and in that role early acquired a place in Christian symbolism. In *Physiologus* it is described as a destroyer of the devil. On the other side of the font, there is a relief of men and dragons. Two dragons are seen tangling with each other, while in each case the tail is in the grasp of a man whose body is out of sight. One of these men clutches at the throat of the other monster with his free hand, while his companion's right hand clasps the foreleg of a unicorn whose foot appears to be planted on his own head. Both men are bearded and have long plaited pigtails. No definite interpretation has been offered as to what these figures represent, although they have often been viewed as incarnations of the Christian God or pagan demons or as a merging of paganism and Christianity.

Similar enigmas arise in the case of a skillfully carved relief in Holzkirchen church near Würzburg, Franconia. In the seclusion of a small village in the Spessart region, amid picturesque ruins of Romanesque monastery, a small structure by Balthazar Neumann, the Würzburg master of Baroque architecture, stands on the site of the former church. Built into it is a stone relief which may have stood as a votive image in the ancient

59. *The Man in the Well* engraved by
B. A. Bolsworth

priory church since the end of the eleventh century. Holzkirchen priory was founded in 775 by one Troandus, supposed to have been high sheriff of the Waldsassen canton. It was later ceded to Charlemagne, who gave the priory to St. Boniface, "the Apostle of the Germans" and bishop of Fulda (Hesse), where a certain unicorn tradition was beginning to develop.

What the unicorn signified in Holzkirchen has not been definitively elucidated. The horseman in flowing cloak in the upper of the two panels may, of course, be identified as Christ on the way to Jerusalem. The inscription reads: *Aequester aedibus in nostris sit tua dextera Christe,* "May thy right hand, o knightly Christ, rest upon our house." No specific inscription applies to the lower panel, where a bearded man is holding a unicorn whose horn curves backward. The church today, rather wary of mysticism, is inclined to identify the bearded man as Troandus, the priory's founder and the unicorn as a symbol of monastic seclusion or as an emblem of the Waldsassen canton where it was said to be a local denizen of the forest. It could even be a memorial to Troandus' son, who was reportedly killed by one. All these interpretations seem a little forced. The unicorn might boldly be interpreted as an image for Christ and the man holding it as God the Father. The unicorn in these circumstances is certainly not simply a monster, and this stone in its most ancient environment may be counted among the loveliest and most exciting German representations of the unicorn. [Ill. 23]

Finally, a comparatively modern example illustrates once again the encounter between lion and unicorn and, like the earlier Freudenstadt font, contains a merging of Christian and non-Christian traditions. It is to be found in the brilliantly painted, barrel-shaped, timbered ceiling of a Jewish house of prayer from Horb-am-Main (Germany). Looking at it gives the impression of entering some enchanted German forest where the unicorn is consorting with the denizens. The unicorn here is fighting the lion and has just pierced his throat with his horn. The painter of this scene, Elieser Susmann, came from what is now the western Ukraine, where traditional Talmudic tales and folklore preserved the notion of the unicorn. In the ceiling, painted in 1735, the lion and the unicorn may well be a reminder of a mutual Judeo-Christian tradition, e.g., Psalm 22, where David is praying for protection against the savage beasts. The Horb tabernacle, which had occasionally been used as a barn, survived every vicissitude after 1914 in the museum at Bamberg until it was exhibited at the great Monumenta Judaica exhibition in Cologne in 1963–64. Because of its tremendous historic importance, it has meantime been transferred to the Israel Museum in Jerusalem. [Ill. 142]

Our brief look at extant' ecclesiastical depictions of the unicorn in

60. Detail from fourteenth-century Syrian glass receptacle

61. Sylvan ass from John Jonston's Bestiary

62. Two varieties of maned unicorn (Jonston)

association with other animals brings us back to the questions raised by the concerned St. Bernard. Perhaps definite meaning eludes us in many examples, but it is clear the stone menagerie offers something beyond "absurd monstrosities" and "formal opulence of shapelessness."

Water unicorn from painted ceiling of church at Zillis (Switzerland), twelfth century

6. The Road to Mysticism

In the twelfth century, the period of St. Bernard and Honorius, lived Hildegard, abbess of Bingen, a mystic also known as the "Sibyl of the Rhine." She recorded many of her mystic visions in the manuscript *Scivias,* and in *Physica,* a book of natural science, is found a version of the capture of the unicorn which is more charming than any before or since. In her story a naturalist studying the animal world could never, to his great surprise, find a unicorn. One day, however, he went on a country outing with a company of men, women, and girls. The younger women wandered away from the main party to amuse themselves among the flowers. A unicorn, catching sight of this group, stops suddenly and sits stock still on his haunches to gaze at the young girls. "When indeed, a unicorn sees a damsel in the distance, he is astonished at the sight of such a beardless being in human form. If, moreover, two or more girls are together, he is still more astonished and can be caught all the more quickly while he sits there staring at them as though petrified." In such circumstances, even our naturalist can approach and seize the stupefied unicorn from behind.

Who could shrug away the charm of so sweet a tale? It is clearly a refined and embellished version of the savage beast especially for nun and novitiates who are taught that entrapment of unicorns is not a job for buxom peasant girls but for daughters of the gentry.

No connection with Christ was forced into this story, but the unicorn nevertheless has something of sacred mystery about it. According to St. Hildegard, its great strength, which makes it superior to all other animals, is due to its going once yearly into the country where the waters of paradise flow. There it seeks out the best herbs and vegetables, paws them loose from the soil, and devours them. When otherwise seen from naturalistic and medical viewpoints, the animal has some trace certainly of the alchemy emanating from Arabia based on the "four humors." Hippocratic pathology defined those four fundamental humors as blood coming from the heart and representing heat, phlegm from the brain representing cold, yellow bile from the liver for dryness, and black bile from spleen and stomach for wetness. For the Pneumatists, on the other hand, blood was the hot, moist humor, phlegm the cold, moist humor, yellow bile the hot, dry humor, and black bile the cold, dry humor.

Hildegard's unicorn is "hot rather than cold." Of course, hot and cold were deemed incompatible, but Hildegard seems to regard those qualities as mixed together in the unicorn. Hildegard's successors in the nunneries cherished the unicorn as part of their adoration of the Virgin, but they may also have deeply felt in it a mystic communion with their Redeemer. They embroidered the sacred beast on vestments, wove it into altar frontals and refectory cloths, and stitched it on pillow covers. The adoration and love of the Brides of Christ for their Lord produced a symbol and substitute which also embodied a sublimation of the mystic bond. There are no accounts of any reactions exceeding pathological bounds, something which was by no means foreign in cloistered atmospheres. Employing the unicorn as symbol of Christ divests the creature of crude reality and etherealizes the mystic bond. [Ills. 36, 56]

While the world of scholasticism, true to the attitude of its master Aristotle, was concerned with precise academic portrayal of the unicorn, mysticism contemporaneously rediscovered in the unicorn the sacred token for Christ. Both viewpoints could be housed in the same individual. Honorius himself, who described the unicorn in its Indian fairyland, also wrote a widely used miscellany of sermons to serve less learned or less diligent confratres not so capable of sustaining the burdens of their offices. In that *Speculum ecclesiae* ("Mirror of the Church") is an address for the Feast of the Annunciation, the first part of which contains various prophetic utterances dealing with this particular event. That section, considerately labelled "for optional use" by Honorius, contains the story of the capture of the unicorn by the maiden. "Christ is represented by this beast, His invincible might by its horn. Just as the animal is taken in the Virgin's lap by the hunters, so is He found in human form by those who love him."

Here the old allegory of *Physiologus* is revived to become an element of the sermon and, like the secular account from India, it becomes a pattern for the plastic arts. During the Middle Ages, as architects and artists were hewing and painting their illustrations of the Bible in the stones and murals of churches, the unicorn continued as a hieroglyph for Christ. It was a sacred seal which even illiterates could recognize and classify properly in meaning and importance. Honorius, who rather than an original, creative personality was more of a compiler like Aelian the Italian, united in his writings the unicorn's lifelines. Thus, it now set foot with symbolic authority within the very precincts of the Church.

Albertus Magnus, the great theologian, was certainly a more important scholar than Honorius. Even when he discarded the naturalistic, scholastic view of the unicorn and introduced its figure into the ecclesiastic theory of the universe, he did so warily and with due scientific care. He seeks his sanction from the Bible and uses Biblical quotations to illustrate his notion of the unicorn as a symbol of Christ, as a creature in whose being the forceful, impatient, and indeed wrathful side is deeply imprinted:

> *This unicorn is Christ whose might, typified by its horn, is irresistible. Thus, in this connection, Isaiah 2:23 ends with the words "Cease ye from man, whose breath is in his nostrils: for wherein is he to be accounted of!" and the psalm tells us he is as beloved as the offspring of unicorns; of which Numbers 23:22 (Luther's version) also states that his joyousness is as the joyousness of the unicorn. Jewish unicorns, particularly faithful to the law, were the ascendants of Mary and her son, the only-begotten of God, the Father who said, according to Matthew 3:17: "This is my beloved son." This unicorn appeared wild and unruly when, at the mere thought of Lucifer's arrogance, it drove Adam out of the Garden of Eden for biting the apple, and destroyed the original world with the Flood. Thus also did it destroy the Sodomites with hellfire and brimstone. Thus did that unicorn rampage in heaven and on earth until our glorious Virgin accepted it into her lap when it entered her citadel, that is to say into the womb of her chaste body so that she could nurse it in her bosom and drape it with modest flesh, wherein in accordance with divine decree the unseizable creature might be captured by its hunters, namely by Jews and Gentiles, and yield voluntarily to death by crucifixion. Thus for example, in Job 39:9-24 "Will the unicorn be willing to serve thee or abide by thy crib? Canst thou bind the unicorn with his hand in the furrow? . . . He swalloweth the ground with fierceness and rage." Thus Christ died from the rage he felt against sinners.*

As a sign of the high medieval revival of *Physiologus,* whose christological interpretation of the unicorn hunt persists alongside the materially, quite skeptically retold narration or even exults over it, this scene was abundantly adopted by the plastic arts in the many variants available: as a calmly contented association and as a hard pursuit to the death. From Latin versions accessible only to the learned, the *Physiologus* fables penetrated almost explosively into the European languages and thence into still wider circles. They were clearly spiced by the whimsical events of the charmingly natural manner of narration and the pervading ethico-Christian commentaries. From literati, the stories certainly travelled by word of mouth and repetition into the general population; it is not necessary to suppose that every craftsman engaged in the reproduction of the *Physiologus* animal kingdom in churches and abbeys had necessarily read the original book! And although their hands were undoubtedly guided by clerics, it is frequently

81

The Virgin Mary with the Unicorn

65.   In Maulbronn choirstall
◁

66.   In Cismar priory church

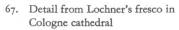

67.   Detail from Lochner's fresco in
      Cologne cathedral

68. On a keystone of St. Stephen's Church, Vienna

83

69. Savage woman and unicorn on choirstall in Konstanz Minster

70. On opposite side of pew from Fig. 69: Savage woman caught in thicket and threatened by demons (Detail)

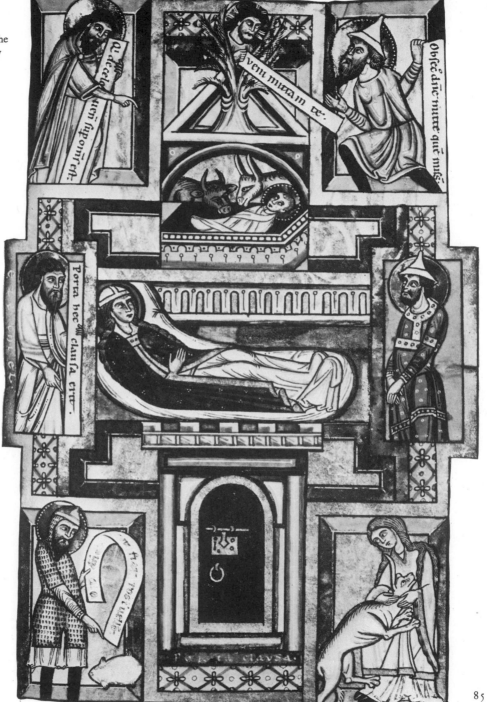

71. Christmas icon with symbols of the
Virgin Mary. Mid-twelfth-century
(unicorn at lower right)

Mystic Unicorn Hunt

72. Lower Rhineland fifteenth-century
▽ tapestry showing Gabriel and Mary
in conversation

73. Unicorn altar at Erfurt cathedral.
▷ *Ca.* 1420, one of the earliest
representations of the Holy Hunt
motif

PORTA CLAVSA

PORTA EZICHIELIS

VIRGA AARON

SI STRTIO OVA EX CVBARE VALET

ARCHADNI

VRSA EETVM ORE FIGVRAT

ORTVS CONCLVSVS

OPV

GLORIA OPVS HOC FIERI FECERVNT NOBILES ET GENEROSI

4. Falconetto's fresco with mystic unicorn hunt in Church of St. Peter the Martyr, Verona. Sixteenth century. (Detail)

5. Fresco with mystic unicorn hunt. Church of Our Lady, Memmingen, *ca.* 1460-1470

76. Fifteenth-century tapestry from Basel,
▽ with symbolic beasts (wild bear, lion,
    unicorn, stag).

77. Feminine cunning. Capital of column
▷ from St. Peter's Church in Caen
    (Normandy). Detail: Virgil in the
    basket, and unicorn hunt

78. Damsel with unicorn. Detail from a
▷ Basel tapestry

79. Rhenish trinket casket from latter half
of fifteenth century. Queen of the
Savages mounted on a unicorn

80. Female savage with unicorn. Late
fifteenth-century Strassburg tapestry
(chairback cover)

hard to decide in a particular case whether a scene is intended to portray something spiritual or profane, say Our Lord's Passion or simply a hunt, a love idyll or an allegory on the Conception. Conception—meaning that the incident is to be seriously taken in the sense of a mystic identity of the image and the meaning. Of course some aids for the interpretation are offered by the surroundings and the contiguous figures, but considering the closely juxtaposed or practically coincident spiritual and mundane existence in medieval man, the context may be deceptive.

There is a clearly religious meaning in the slaying of the unicorn on a quatrefoil in the choirstall of Cologne cathedral; even the influence of oriental style in the apparel of the hunter who is dispatching the animal with his bow and arrow seems to indicate that this scene is intended to portray the death of Christ. The frequently depicted scene appears also on a misericord in Trinity Church, Stratford-on-Avon, England. Shakespeare was buried in that churchyard, and it is almost certain that he had seen that carving during his lifetime, for he mentions the beast many a time in his works, albeit with a touch of enlightened skepticism. [Ills. 47, 48]

In contrast, there is a portrayal of the unicorn slaughter generally held to be purely profane by contemporary science. But it is particularly impressive and its power of attraction makes this hard to believe. The piece in question is a small, circular, strikingly colored, silver-enamel salver from a fourteenth century Rhenish (or conceivably French) atelier now in the Bavarian National Museum, Munich. The hunter is standing on a tree and thrusting his spear through the nape of a powerfully drawn beast whose knees are giving way. The maiden is still clasping its long straight horn, and in her raised right hand she holds a circular object which reappears in other representations. Its meaning is unclear. If we regard the subject purely as mundane, and that could apply for example to a set of Parisian trinket boxes showing the unicorn hunt alongside a scene from *Tristram and Iseult,* one might think the object was a garland which the maiden is handing to the victor. The interpretation of the circular object as the Holy Grail into which Christ's blood dripped is not too convincing. On the Munich silver tray, this item could be a mirror; the spotless mirror is one of the symbols of the Virgin Mary, who is the unsullied glass in which God saw his own image for the first time. [Ills. 44, 46]

The step into mystic understanding of the hunting scene was described in literature with particular clarity by a man who had himself undergone a mystic experience, although not necessarily with this particular object. Conrad of Megenberg (1309–1374), prebendary of Regensburg cathedral, experienced a miraculous cure during a mass in which two anthems composed by him were being sung. Though he had lived previously in

82. Detail from *Defensorium virginitatis* (Compurgation of the Marian Virginity)

95

Paris and Vienna, Regensburg is the city where he remains respected as a pillar of the church, where on occasion he acted as mediator to the Antipope at Avignon on behalf of the Abbey of St. Emmeran. His popular *Book of Nature,* reputably the first natural history text in German, was largely responsible for the fifteenth century becoming immediately the Age of the Unicorn in Germany. Conrad relates the story along the lines of Gregory and Isidore but with embellishments of his own which prove he had studied the matter more deeply than either of his predecessors. In the maiden's presence the unicorn forgets all his fury "and honors the purity of her chaste, coy body by laying his head in her lap and falling asleep then and there." Thus the hunters capture the beast "and take it into the royal palaces to be put on show and exhibited to the populace," just as Megasthenes had described unicorn colts being taken into the king's presence and exhibited in gala performances. Conrad applied this to Christ, who, after ascending to the palace of the King of Heaven, "Vouchsafed a seraphic appearance to the host of all the Saints and Angels." But Christ is also the unicorn because "before becoming man, he harbored wrath and fury against the vanity of the angels and against the stubbornness of the people on earth." The change from fury to meekness found by Gregory the Great in Saul-become-Paul is here applied to the Savior himself. Those "heavenly hosts" that brought the unknown author of *Physiologus* under the suspicion of gnosticism are here carefully placed in the correct canonic hierarchy as angels.

The intimate, peaceful communion of maiden and unicorn – we may now say of Mother and Child – without any menacing hunters about became particularly dear to Germans. On a medallion on the altar at Cismar in Holstein there is an austere, bolt upright Virgin. The finest keystone of St. Stephen's cathedral in Vienna is enhanced by the Virgin in the form of a buxom rustic beauty; on the choirstall in Maulbronn Abbey, the best preserved medieval cloister in Germany, located in the Black Forest, the Virgin is an entrancing vision. Hassocks originally from Cologne show the maid and unicorn corralled inside a strong border or thicket of thorn, safe in their miniature garden of Eden with lilies of the valley and other compatible blooms while nettles grow in the wicked world on the outside. On Stefan Lochner's Epiphany altar in Cologne cathedral, the maid is wearing a breast ornament for fastening her cloak. This brooch has a pearl and precious stone inlay of the Virgin and the unicorn, again therefore the Mother and Child now indicating His supernatural origin. None of the worshippers can detect that detail; the image is too far off. There it is in front of everybody's eyes yet seen by none – truly a "sacred open secret." [Ills. 36, 64, 65, 66, 67, 68]

Though associated with the Virgin Mary, the unicorn is occasionally connected with other holy women, especially those whose chastity is meant to be glorified, such as St. Justine. A Gobelin tapestry at Trübau in Moravia shows our beast in the retinue of the Queen of Sheba. In St. Michael's Church, commanding a view of the Susa valley west of Turin (Italy), a sixteenth-century fresco depicts John the Baptist in the wilderness preaching to the animals, among which is a white unicorn. A 1545 Gobelin at Langres Cathedral, France, dedicated to St. Mammes, includes a unicorn among the other creatures listening to that saint's sermon.

The unicorn may thus be an embodiment of virtue or a symbol for Christ or, for example, a standing guard over human saints such as Stephen on a Gobelin in the Cluny Museum, Paris; the exquisite creature has become a useful and potent part of Church language, written or artistic. [Ills. 126, 126a]

83. Sixteenth century, from Spain

7. The Celestial Hunt

Sinu matris conditur,   *Unfetter'd by the world—at rest,*
Qui mundo non clauditur,   *Peaceful on the mother's breast.*
Pietate trahitur,   *By his artless trust betrayed,*
Utero concluditur,   *In the trap her bosom made,*
Unicornis capitur.   *Such is the Unicorn's arrest!*

From an ancient missal at Neuhausen near Pforzheim (Germany)

Just before the middle of the thirteenth century, the ruling house of Babenberg (which had been dominant since 936 in what is now Austrian territory) was at the point of extinction with the death of the childless duke Frederick II, and many a hand was undoubtedly ready to seize his estates. Among these was the abbey of Göss in the southeast Austrian province of Styria. Cunigund the abbess, in her temporal and seignorial capacity, had many concerns, but these apparently were no hindrance to her spiritual zeal and genius for religious creation. Among the works of art produced at Göss under her direction (for it is doubtful whether her many duties ever gave her time to set her own needle to the work) is a frontal bearing the inscription CHUNEGUNDIS ABATISSA ME FECIT, "Abbess Cunigund made me." Among the sumptuous cloths and priestly vestments made by the sisters of the convent, this ideological document is an outstanding example of the high quality of late Romanesque handicraft. The unexcelled embroidery of silk completely covering the linen ground in lustrous colors of brilliant yellow and deep blue affects the visitor most impressively even now. It is a remarkable and unique precursor of a group of motifs which two hundred years later singularly expressed the German mystic cult for Christ and the Virgin Mary. [Ill. 56]

The unicorn frequently appears on the priestly vestments from Göss, in company with and of equal standing with the other ornamentation. On the antependium or altar frontal before us it occupies a central position in the familiar representation of the Annunciation. The angel approaches the Virgin and greets her "Hail Mary . . ." and between these two figures is a little unicorn, graceful as a thoroughbred, with distinctly cloven hoofs. It is as though, at this instant of the Annunciation, the person so heralded was himself leaping toward the woman who was to be his earthly mother. The dove of the Holy Ghost hovers over the three of them. That much abused word "unique" does seem fitting here; we know of no other representation that expresses the essence of the matter with such delicate and sensitive restraint. The whole meaning of the composition is indicated in utmost conciseness and stylization, the symbolic content of the two animal figures being obvious. It was not mere chance that this work originated in a convent. The beast, which is amenable to virginal purity, became a symbol and a mystic incorporation to the nuns of their love for Christ. Cunigund herself was probably well acquainted with the original German edition of *Physiologus* and thus was able to combine into one image with a bold hand the love of Christ and the cult of the Virgin that was spreading into the occident from the east.

This cult was already finding literary expression during the twelfth century. Religious poetry, such as the *Marienlied,* the Melk Abbey hymn to the Virgin, contains these symbols: the Burning Bush where Moses, like Mary much later, was submissive to the call of the Lord; the Closed Portal of Ezekiel through which "the king passed gloriously in and out"; and Gideon's Fleece, which "God sprinkled with his celestial dew" as he did with Mary. (These two quotations are from Walther von der Vogelweide's *Poem to the Trinity*.) These symbols appear together around 1140 in a missal for St. Michael's Abbey at Hildesheim (near Hanover). The scene is the first Noel: Mary stands in the center beneath the manger, surrounded by those prophetic indications of virgin birth. Joseph with his peaked Jewish hat is also a part of the setting. "Since he took care of her, it is thereby testified that she remained an unsullied virgin," in the words of Giacopo da Voragine. In one of those pictures, however, the closeness of Virgin and unicorn is again testimony for the supernaturality of this birth. [Ill. 71]

Before the final artistic imagery evolved, the mystic hunt was given form by religious poetry. The Son of God is in the beginning unready to become mortal and to suffer as a man, as is required of him. He has to be coerced, nay, compelled to the task. Christ the unicorn is chased by the hunter God-Father and then by Gabriel, at the latter's command, who drives him into the Virgin's lap. The slaying of the unicorn was an ancient symbol for Christ's martyrdom. Thus the unicorn hunt becomes a celestial event and at the same time an image of the Annunciation and Conception within the earthly body. This Christian, mystic unicorn hunt mingles with pagan traditions, with the role of the "Wild Huntsman" who thunders through the fall nights over hill and dale, forest and fell. In more recent times, the "Wild Hunt" has been known in some Westphalian localities as the "angelic steeplechase," and in the Midlands shire of Stafford in England, "Gabriel's Hounds."

This spiritual chase culminates in the *Hortus conclusus,* the "garden inclosed" of the Song of Solomon, which harbors the mother of God, in many other forms as a bower, a bed of rosebushes, a garland, or a hedge—a dual symbol, as it not only offers the Virgin protection against the world but also signifies according to the Old Testament her own bosom in which she carries and shelters the Child. This garden becomes the scene of the Annunciation. The archangel Gabriel appears in the vestments of a deacon, as a hunter with spear and hunting horn (rarely with a scepter instead of his weapon or with the horn alone). He leads his pack on the leash, and only exceptionally do any of his hounds run free.

The Virgin sits in the garden, her hair unbound as a token of virginity, and in her lap she shelters the beast which the angel has been hunting – the unicorn. The object of the chase was not to slay the animal but to drive it into the Virgin's bosom. So, Gabriel the Hunter raises his spear instead of driving it home, and, setting his horn to his lips, he sounds the mort. Annunciation and Conception are completed at one blow. Inside the garden, outside it, and by the wall or fence surrounding it are a number of prophetic allusions to the coming of Christ and the Virgin birth; there are considerably more of them than were found in that early Hildesheim miniature. Frequently, God the Father looks down in benediction from the heavens, sending the Christ child bearing a cross down on a beam of light to his mother, and thus Christ is, so to speak, doubly present in mortal and in spiritual form, if one does not wish to assume that the unicorn is now representing the procreative spirit as the third element of the Trinity. Nevertheless, the dove also is occasionally present. In some portrayals, the child mounted on the unicorn rides toward his mother, and such a plethora of motifs may cast some doubt on whether the old master responsible for the painting was fully aware of its whole meaning. Christian legend, fraught with millennial tradition, a mystic combination of profane and sacred components taken together, converts the representations of the unicorn hunt into a remarkable document of the later Middle Ages – within the conflicting context of folk poetry, sincere belief, and intellectual profundity – as charming as it is, so to speak, ludicrous. [Ill. 75]

Certainly this motif has a unique place in the huge amount of religious iconography which flourished during the two centuries immediately prior to the Reformation.

The unicorn before us now is not bound by definite form or size. It may sometimes look like a toy animal, and elsewhere it can be huge enough to dominate the whole setting. Ram, stag, and horse contributed jointly and individually to its composition. Sometimes the horn looks extremely fragile, but mostly it is straight and strong; it also exhibits the peculiar whorls mentioned by Megasthenes which became an essential unicorn feature in the Middle Ages. The hounds remaining with the hunter outside of the wall sometimes press on with him into the garden and are often depicted by stripes and strokes. They are the symbols for Christian virtues, and there is a certain amount of irony in the iconoclast Bernard of Clairvaux having been the source of the concept for this particular symbolism. His annotations to Psalm 85 contain a parable of those virtues and their conflict in regard to iniquitous mankind. Truth and Righteousness voted to condemn Man, Placidity and Compassion pleaded in his behalf—finally all are united by Christ for the work of redemption. These virtues are not always four in number. According to the mind's eye of the artist or his patron, probably also for reasons of space, there may be three or two or occasionally only one hound. Sometimes, though, out of the mundane hunt the gun dog appears as an additional fifth, its duty being to start the game. [Ills. 72, 73]

The Marian symbols, to which we have already referred in passing, arose from the Song of Songs and other portions of the Old Testament, and occasionally additional symbols of Christ are introduced from *Physiologus*, namely the lion, pelican, and phoenix. This portion of the iconography probably owes its existence to a remarkable book by the Viennese Dominican, Professor Francis de Resza (from Retz on the Enns); namely *Defensorium inviolatae virginitatis Mariae* ("Defence of the Intact Virginity of Mary"), a thesis founded on accounts of miracles, each of which invariably conclude with "If that was then feasible, why should it not . . ." Picture and text illustrate the various events, such as how King Xerxes's wine turned into blood, how the bird Bonafa mates by osculation (one item which had already been labeled fable by Albertus Magnus), and "Virginal purity can trap the unicorn. Thus was a virgin able even to conceive the Son of God." "Rhinoceros" was the term used in the original Latin text, but the illustration shows the now conventional figure of the unicorn. To each of these fragments of nonsense its source of "authentication" is added, especially ancient writers and Church Fathers. In the case of the unicorn, its witnesses are St. Isidore of Seville (about 600) and Alanus ab Insulis (Alan of Lille), a tasteful, erudite twelfth-century poet–though what could he have contributed to the uncouth debate which he is here called upon to serve! [Ill. 35]

Francis of Resza died in 1425 and about that time or shortly thereafter, the picture now regarded as the oldest extant example of the sacred hunt was painted. This was the central panel for an altar of prothesis at Weimar, now in the museum of that city. Search in Thüringen for the source of the weird, legendary symbolism brought to light a whole series of specimens, and the popular subject of the mystic unicorn hunt appears to have spread out from there to all parts of Germany. It was executed in a tremendous variety of art forms, as paintings, altar carvings, woven in antependia and other tapestries, patches sewn on to a groundwork, and occasionally in bookcovers and other craftwares. [Ills. 72, 73, 85, 117]

Apart from graphic and minor skilled handicrafts, a still undoubtedly incomplete survey leaves us with some seventy major works showing the sacred hunt now known. Much meantime has certainly perished or been destroyed. The number of locations is small because at various times several works were produced in one place (for example, the motif about which we are speaking here was a special favorite in the nunneries of Lower Saxony). Of the works of art now preserved in museums, origins in many cases remain not fully authenticated. On the whole, however, these items do give some idea as to where the mystic unicorn hunt enjoyed special favor. The motif did not develop solely in Germany but continued broadly dominant wherever German culture penetrated. There appear to be two somewhat loosely associated zones of that culture. One of these centered in Thüringen, where the former kingdom and the earlier province of Saxony became one, and some ramifications range thence toward Silesia; northward, lower Saxony joins in sending its influence toward Brandenburg, Mecklenburg and Holstein, and thus into Denmark. One may well assume that an obviously fairly late painted ceiling in the church at Hattula in Finland may have been inspired from across the Baltic.

A second extensive area of the mystic unicorn hunt covers the upper Rhineland plain and the alpine regions; between the Vosges mountains and the Black Forest, the unicorn was greatly favored in yet another form. A painting from Schongauer's studio and now in the Unterlinden Museum at Colmar is credited with some influence in the dissemination of the sacred unicorn hunt motif. One workshop on the central Rhine appears to have manufactured various antependia with the unicorn hunt and to have supplied these to churches during several decades. In the southern Alps, Tyrol, and Carinthia, a few samples are also to be found.

With full Renaissance pomp, the prodigy made its way into the church of St. Peter the Martyr in Verona. Here, next to other Old Testament prophecies, the Gideon miracle takes a central position. The Virgin is like a Christian Danae, with the Child descending toward her in a downpour from the presence of God the Father; Gideon stands outside the Virgin's bower, the *Hortus conclusus,* and the legend reads "He descends like rain upon my fleece." [Ill. 74]

It was in Switzerland that this type of painting had its most remarkable development. Toward the middle of the sixteenth century, in the reformed region of the Swiss Confederation, tapestries were produced that again adopted the motif that was offensively superstitious to Protestant eyes and were even embellished with a variant. Now Adam and Eve enter the *Hortus conclusus*. Carriers of original sin, they first made the act of redemption a necessity. That is strikingly represented by Adam driving his javelin into the breast of the unsuspecting unicorn while Eve collects the blood in a basin, a throwback to an enigmatic, especially French motif. Four such tapestries are now in the Swiss National Museum in Zurich.

No wonder there were reservations about the substance of those Swiss tapestries, which were even the subject of a specially directed theological verdict. Among the Reformers Luther, who had already absorbed the unicorn into his translation of the Bible and to whom mystic frenzy was nothing extraordinary, inveighed violently against such pictures. Luther rampaged against one work especially: the Grimmenthal *Vallem furoris* ("Valley of wrath"). The portrayal of the hunt on a unicorn altar in the Lower Saxon abbey of Grimmenthal was credited with miraculous powers and attracted streams of pilgrims. It was said to cure the maimed, the halt, the blind, cripples, paralytics, and even syphilitics, and reputedly 44,000 people visited it in a year. The artist, Paul Lautensack (Master Paul of Bamberg), who spent ten years on the masterpiece and further decorations in the abbey, is said to have earned the enormous sum of 12,000 florins for his labors. He reportedly died a fanatic Protestant in 1558 at Nuremberg. By that time, Grimmenthal had ceased to be a shrine for pilgrims. In 1767 the house of God with Master Paul's paintings was destroyed by fire.

The Church had long since drawn away from naive belief in miracles. At its twenty-fifth session on December 3 and 4, 1563, the Council of Trent passed a resolution covering the invocation, adoration, and relics of saints and sacred images. Images and icons of Christ, the Mother of God and other sainted beings were henceforth still to enjoy respect and veneration, but not because they might be of divine character or because some favor might be solicited from them "or because people might place their trust in images just as in former times tribes had placed their hopes on idols," but because the original paintings of such representations were worthy of honor. All supersition in the invocation of saints was henceforth to cease; all wicked traffic was to be eliminated, and especially, all lewdness was to be avoided. The installation of unusual portrayals was in future to be subject to the approval of the bishops. Introduced in a prudent and conservative manner, this was still a condemnation of the fetishism which had become so dear to medieval mankind. A facet of the Reformation thus was fulfilled; reform was after all the task of the Council of Trent. The representation of the unicorn, though not explicitly mentioned in the Trent resolution, was virtually regarded as one of the "unusual portrayals." It became rare, and the mystic hunt vanished from sight. Stripping away myth deprived the Church of some of its charm, and even those who appreciate the historic need governing that decision cannot fail to be slightly saddened at this turn of events. The Verdict of Trent appears to have aftereffects even to this day. Some Catholic scholars severely condemn the mystic unicorn imagery as tasteless. But others, such as G. M. Dreves, a Jesuit, see it as one of the finest triumphs of symbolism. "With the medieval predilection for this equally pensive and popular code language, there is no need to wonder if such representation enjoyed special favor," he says. "Not only with the artificers themselves but also with the people."

Indeed the people had an affectionate attachment to this myth, which was reflected not only in literature but also in popular poetry and fiction. This may go back further than can be verified with any certainty nowadays. Such connection was produced certainly earlier in literature than in pictorial art. We are indebted for such expression to Master Heinrich of Meissen known as Frauenlob, born around 1250, and the Franconian Conrad of Würzburg, who lived many years in Basel in the thirteenth century, both early specimens of a new profession: the writer. In their works and in early folksongs possibly based on formal poetry, it is still God the Father himself who drives his son into Mary's bosom. Is there some vestige of Odin in this?

Later, the Lord orders his archangel to take up the hunt. Thus, in one of the folksongs collected by Ludwig Uhland:

A huntsman will a-hunting go,
He's starting from the throne of Heav'n.
What's this encounter'd on the way?
Mary the Virgin, 'tis indeed.
The huntsman whom I mean,
To us is known his fame.
With an angel goes he hunting;
Gabriel's his very name.
The angel blows his tiny horn,
Ev'ry note is well in place;
Greeting to thee, O Mary,
For thou art full of grace.

In thy child, thy father's hid,
Thy mother and thy nurse are same,
The unicorn and now the kid,
Both of them hath she made tame.

Again, in a Christmas carol by chaplain Heinrich of Laufenburg, later deacon of Freiburg, the unicorn enters:

> *The unicorn, it's just been caught*
> *In maiden's lap, by cunning thought,*
> *And – 't was Jesus Christ!*
> *O Mary, that's thy due,*
> *And worth thou well hast earn'd,*
> *The stag with thee has sheltered*
> *Thou tender, pretty doe.*

Clearly but one more step remains: for the mystic bond between mother and son to become identity through the agency of the unicorn. To the Christ of the spirit of the unicorn, there comes as a final step in the German mystic adoration of the Virgin the appellation of the mother of God as *Maria unicornis* (Mary of the unicorn).

In Protestant hymnals around the middle of the sixteenth century, there were some unicorn lyrics presumably permissible for singing in church. One song taken from the collection *Bergkreyen* ("Mountain songs") dates most probably from the first three decades of the sixteenth century, though it may be even older. Unfortunately, it suffered considerable garbling. In it the stage is set—a pleasant mountain scene with roses and twittering birds—and then it continues roughly as follows:

2. *I heard the song of sweetest nightingale,*
   So well she sang, it echoed through the forest,
   Right 'twixt two mountains and a deep ravine,
   I heard resound full many a noble tone.

3. *The hunter too did note the sound,*
   And boldly hunts the unicorn with much delight,
   That unicorn proudly noble, proudly highborn,
   For God himself had chosen him.

4. *The unicorn, by nature, and white as well,*
   Straight and ready there he blocks the narrow path,
   No mortal man there is can trap him there,
   But yet a virgin pure could do it.

5. *Were this unicorn for us not born,*
   Then all we sinners'd be forlorn.
   Unworthily, then, we take him in,
   God help us all into his father's realm,
   God save us all the same!

Here now is the unicorn fully developed into its conventional form in the western world: white, noble, unseizable, to be entrapped only by a spotless **virgin**, symbol also for the Son of God. Independent from natural and historic prototypes, this unicorn is an artistic production of the human mind.

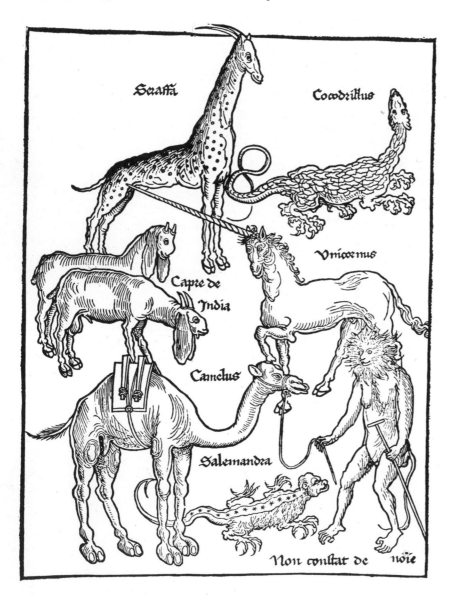

84. Animals of the Holy Land, in von Breydenbach's travel book. Woodcut by Erhard Reuwich, end of fifteenth century

85. Detail with unicorn hunt, from late fifteenth-century altar frontal from Gelnhausen (Hesse, West Germany)

Dns Angelus Corrario de Venetijs deinde Gregorius xij electus anno dm m̄
cccc vj sedit annis circa y ꝓ & priuatus p Conciliū pisanum anno dm M
cccc viiij legatus Marchie anconitan̄ mortuus & sepultus in Recaneto

Duplicem tritiui i̇ em auis apies cruciſera auis requiris cornuger ſunt milicij
veloces ſint pp. Laſaūas principum hns vnitatem & finem vnitati duplici vo
caconis vnius reuirue figure multomagis minū extremū ſic in tp̄e boni anni
venit dies inqua tenebit in mediate airuate figure multomagis quidam rex
volucrum ſolus em reapiens principium medie inquo explebit cornuto die
mediante stella poli & pp tumultum & felix exns ad bella paratus o gentis
brzanaꝗ hns auditis nobis inclinatos & ignis ſine frenis o amice f vltima
ſilli ml luciabz te i loas irriguis pp ſpem cadens mte principatū & finis cornu ee

Penitentia veſtigia Symonis magi tenebit

86. The picture of the Pope with the
unicorn appears in all editions of the
so-called Papal Prophecies of Joachim
of Fiore.

8. Eye Witnesses

Of the accounts by people claiming to have seen the unicorn, two are particularly significant, not only because they give a minute description but because they both emanate from men of the cloth and ought therefore to be trustworthy. Both originate from the Holy Land, both from pilgrims who were able to travel there after the crusades were over.

One of these writers, a Dutch priest, Johannes van Hesse of Utrecht, was in Palestine in 1389 when he saw the Water Prodigy: "Near the field Helyon in the Promised Land is the river Marah, whose bitter waters Moses made sweet with a stroke from his staff and the children of Israel drank thereof. To this day, it is said, malicious animals poison this water after sundown, so that none can thereupon drink any longer from the stream. But early in the morning, as soon as the sun rises, a unicorn comes out of the ocean, dips his horn into the stream and drives out the venom from it so that the other animals may drink thereof during the day. This, as I describe it, I saw with my own eyes." What a confirmation of his Grecian predecessors! What encouragement for all those artists who repeatedly portrayed the mythical incident as a symbol for absolution of sin-corrupted mankind! And what evidence of the power of a horn which was to be employed pharmaceutically for hundreds of years! (see Exodus 15:23–25).

Not until a century later was Hesse's story printed in Cologne. The elegant incunabulum is no more than a page and a half of demy octavo, but what a great deal that traveler recorded – even the walls of Paradise itself! Only toward the end of the nineteenth century was one learned scholar bold enough to assert that Hesse had never even left his native Utrecht.

In 1483 Bernard of Breydenbach, deacon at Mainz, and a certain Count Solms (youngest in years in the traveling party, but inferior to none in noble mettle) were joined by a number of companions in a pilgrimage to Palestine. Among the others was the chaplain Friar Felix Faber of Zurich, and as their illustrator the Dutchman Erhard Reuwich, a draftsman, blockmaker, and printer. It was he who published in Mainz Breydenbach's travel book, providing it with woodcuts that, in the opinion of experts, "are not only the largest in format but also technically the most perfect from the age of incunabula." The book appeared in both Latin and German. Also, Chaplain Faber, who had now made two journeys to Palestine, was persuaded by the persistence of his colleagues in the Dominican monastery at Ulm to allow his thrilling anecdotes to be printed. These volumes give a sparkling picture of oriental travel during a comparatively peaceful period when the flow of travelers bent on pilgrimage was increasing steadily.

Crowds of people from various west European countries gathered in Venice, where our little group concluded a contract with a certain Italian Count Reni. The journey to Jerusalem and back cost forty-two ducats a head including two meals a day (with liquor) and lodging. At landing places on the way, the ship was not to moor for more than two or three days at a time for the charterer's other business matters. Anyone who decided after arriving in Jerusalem to travel on to the famous abbey of St. Catherine on Mount Sinai and thence to Egypt—thus relinquishing the return trip—was guaranteed a refund of ten florins. Every obligation was faithfully fulfilled, and the travelers were particularly pleased with the care and attention they received in the Holy Land itself, where they felt themselves at a disadvantage on account of the language barrier and their helplessness among the Arabs.

After a fairly long sojourn in Jerusalem, the travelers joined a new group which now came to an agreement with an Arabian entrepreneur for the further journey through St. Catherine's to Cairo. This too was a package deal, twenty-three ducats from Jerusalem through Sinai up to Gazara oasis near Cairo. However, the travelers had to bear the cost of wine out of their own pockets, for a strictly orthodox Moslem could not properly be expected to defile himself in that respect. Other extra-package demands were made after the stay at St. Catherine's abbey, and finally even the Christian seamen on whom they relied in Alexandria for the return journey made exorbitant demands on them before the homeward voyage.

What happened on the twentieth day after the departure of the caravan from Jerusalem is significant. They reached a bleak mountain chain where the only vegetation was thorny thickets just blossoming to refresh the pilgrims with their perfume. It was said that Christ's crown of thorns had been woven from such branches and so the pilgrims began to pluck token twigs. They were thus already in mystic rapport when suddenly they saw a strange animal in the sterile landscape of red- and black-streaked rocks. Friar Faber has given a precise description of the phenomenon:

> *Toward noon we spotted an animal gazing down at us from a mountain peak. We thought it was a camel and wondered how a camel might remain alive in the wilderness, and this speculation raised a discussion among us as to whether there might also be forest camels. Our guide Kalin approached us, however, and stated that the animal must certainly be a*

87. Detail from *The Quadrupeds*.
Eighteenth century, Spain

rhinoceros or a unicorn, and he pointed out to us the single horn which jutted from the animal's forehead. With great caution we gazed back at this most noble creature, regretting that it was no closer for us to examine it still more minutely. For in many respects this is quite a peculiar animal. In particular, it is said to be very savage. It has a single horn about four-foot long, so pointed and strong that it injures or bores right through anything it meets and nails it to the rocks. Also, its horn has a magical brilliance; fragments of it are as treasured as the most precious stones and are mounted in gold and silver. The animal is so wild that no artifice or cleverness of the hunter avails to catch it, but natural scientists assure us that he may be caught by placing a chaste maiden in his path. As he races towards her she exposes her bosom and he lies down there, bereft of all wildness and so bemused that he stays defenseless against the hunters' spears which now can slay him. If, however, they wish to take him alive, force will be unavailing since he would die on the spot from chagrin under such circumstances, for he is an intractable creature. He is so strong that the Holy Writ (Numbers 23) compares the strength of God himself with that of the unicorn, and so intractable is he that in Job 19 asks "Canst thou bind the unicorn with his hand in the furrow . . ." David speaks of the unicorn in terms both good and bad. It is a mighty animal having the body of a horse, the feet of an elephant and the tail of a hog. In color it resembles boxwood and it utters a fearsome roar. It fights and vanquishes the elephant by thrusting its horn through the softer tissues of its adversary. As previously mentioned, it is miraculously fond of unspoiled maidens. Albertus Magnus in his book on animals relates that Pompey the Great brought a unicorn to Rome for exhibition.

We rested for some time at the bottom of the mountain where the animal stood regarding us as pleasantly as we regarded it, for it stood still and moved not until we had gone on our way.

Unconcerned about Megasthenes's description, wherever Faber took it from, **Erhard Reuwich depicted the unicorn in the form of a horse on the** same sheet as other animals and flatly stated underneath the picture "These animals are faithfully portrayed just as we observed them in the Holy Land." And yet he was a scrupulous reporter. Near his drawing of a man with a lion's head, he wrote "We know not what he is called." [Ill. 84]

How then could the unicorn, in view of these and similar eyewitness evidences, have been drowned in the Deluge or have become extinct since that catastrophe? Indeed, bones have been unearthed when tilling the ground or excavating on a large scale for mining operations. In 1663, one specimen came to light in a limestone cave in the neighborhood of

Quedlinburg, north of the Harz mountains in Lower Saxony. This caused quite a sensation. People flocked to the excavation and many pocketed a few bones as souvenirs; bones there were to spare, for the cave was full of fossil remains. Bitter litigation arose as to the rightful ownership of the property. Finally the abbess of Quedlinburg was able to proceed with methodical excavations, with no less an authority than the famous scientist Otto von **Guericke (known to this day for his experiment with the Magdeburg** hemispheres) undertaking to reconstruct a unicorn skeleton from the debris. This skeleton has only two legs and relies for support on a powerful tail into which its spine merges. And of course there was the horn. The philosopher Leibnitz, who served the Hanoverian princes in several capacities, included this drawing in his posthumously published *Protogaea,* a treatise on the geological antecedents of their provinces. If we look closely enough, we see that he prudently shelved any personal responsibility. [Ill. 88]

A few skeletal fragments found in Russia and Siberia belong to an animal which has been given the scientific name of *Elasmotherium* (literally "armorplated beast"). It was the size of an elephant but rather closer to the rhinoceros in physique, although its nasal region was too weak to have supported a horn. Nevertheless, skulls which have been discovered show an extraordinarily thick osseous pad on the forehead, which was clearly intended to support an immense horn.

It is within reason that this animal might have been exterminated by its human neighbors in Siberia. There are reports that the elasmotherium has been found on rare occasions in the Rhineland, although we have no knowledge of any museum where such remains may have been preserved. Had our primitive ancestors actually seen such a monster, it might indeed have been the source of a primeval conception of the unicorn!

Figura Sceleti prope Quedlinburgum effossi.

88. Reconstructed skeleton of "unicorn" fossils found near Quedlinburg

9. The Costly Horn

When mammoth bones were discovered in 1905 during excavations in the Slovak region of Austria-Hungary, workmen broke off pieces – not as mere souvenirs but to pulverize for use against intermittent fevers; they took them home as remains of unicorn, so long the source of marvelous healing substances. From the China Sea to the Atlantic shores of southwest Europe, the unicorn springs up even into the present, maintaining itself as a medicament, as a restorative for sexual potency, and, with its pronounced phallic shape, also as a vigorous love symbol. An article that appeared in 1922 tells us that children in Asturias (Spain) were still protected against the evil eye when the midwife poured water from a bone beaker called *alicorn*. In Greece, youngsters were protected from the evil eye by a bone cross called *monokero,* and however much philologists seek to derive the word from *monos o kyrios,* "the lord alone (assists)," the common people think only of the single horn, the unicorn. When necessary, other horns have been substituted. One cold winter when the chamois of the southern Alps came down to shelter in the valleys, it is said they were slaughtered in huge numbers solely for their horns which were pulverized to serve as an aphrodisiac, as was the case with Ctesias's wild asses.

Unicorn's horn penetrated the consciousness of the West on its reputation for purging poisons and healing diseases, as built up by Ctesias and Megasthenes and countless others after them. What *Physiologus* understood regarding decontamination of water by making the sign of the cross with the horn confirmed that notion and fortified it with the Christian accent. The curative power of the horn in classical antiquity did not find any practical meaning, since in that epoch there were no unicorns. The Orient did, however, have one – the rhinoceros, whose horn seems to have enjoyed an unbroken tradition right down to our own time as a remedy and as a stimulant to love. In China it is still presumably marketed as a medicament and aphrodisiac, though whether that is feasible in the modern, revolutionary China remains to be seen. In India, the *Unesco Courier* in September 1966 reported, "Slaughter by savages has reduced the stock of single-horned Asian rhinoceros in Kaziranga Game Preserve (Assam) to less than 400. The animal is hunted for its horn, whose supposed yet thoroughly mythical

89. United in 1603, the English lion and Scottish unicorn in the British coat of arms

properties as a medicine and aphrodisiac give it a blackmarket value of one thousand dollars a pound."

Now the rhinoceros did have a certain though indirect effect on the development of European concepts of the unicorn, but it never became *the* European unicorn. This latter acquired its own purely fanciful figure. And its own reality. There were the eyewitness accounts, and there was, as we shall see, the presence of unicorn horns in the later Middle Ages. A quantity of prescriptions was accordingly available, most of them probably transmitted by word of mouth, some in printed form. Arabic alchemy, with its attempts to transmute other elements into gold, had gained a foothold in Europe, pervading general chemistry and medicine, and certainly contributed to this state of affairs.

As mentioned in the chapter "The Road to Mysticism," St. Hildegard of Bingen (1098-1179) wrote that the unicorn is "more hot than cold," referring thereby to one of the great alchemic antitheses for the classification of elements and organisms. In the Latin edition of her works published by Migne, Paris, 1855, unicorn prescriptions are available to us:

> *Take some unicorn liver, grind it up and mash with egg yolk to make an ointment. Every type of leprosy is healed if treated frequently with this ointment, unless the patient is destined to die or God intends not to aid him. For the liver of that animal has a good, pure warmth and the yolk is the most precious part of the egg and like a salve. Leprosy however comes frequently from black bile and from plethoric black blood. Take some unicorn pelt, from it cut a belt and gird it round the body, thus averting attack by plague or fever.*
> *Make also some shoes from unicorn leather and wear them, thus assuring everhealthy feet, thighs and joints, nor will the plague ever attack those limbs.*
> *Apart from that, nothing else of the unicorn is to be used medically.*

A later reviser apparently added: "Anyone who fears being poisoned should place a unicorn hoof beneath the plate containing his food or the mug holding his liquor. If warm food and drink are poisoned, the hoof will make them effervesce; if they are cold, it will make them steam. Thus one can detect whether they are poisoned or not."

Among the cures tried by the knights of the Holy Grail for the arrow wound of Amfortas was the carbuncle that grew beneath the horn of the "monocirius" (recognized also in pastor Lambert's song to Alexander). This remedy was predestined for the suffering monarch of the Grail. Can it be that there are no therapeutic properties at all in the part of a unicorn taken for a carbuncle? St. Hildegard, however, knew nothing about that; she talks not of a gemstone but of a crystal-clear bone (*os*) or, according to another reading, a piece of bronze (*aes*). Surprisingly enough, the Rhenish prioress did not see the miraculous beast's curative power in its most outstanding feature, the horn; to her, the liver and pelt were the most important. Where she acquired her wisdom or whether she perchance misconstrued some Arabian source is still obscure.

By the time of Dr. Conrad Gesner, Zurich (1516-1565), pharmacopoeia had to deal with the problem of adulterated and genuine unicorn horn:

> *The potency of the unicorn is more curative forward near the tip than behind, and care should be taken to buy the whole or at any rate large chunks of the horn, so as to run less risk of trickery. You will find only small fragments in apothecaries' shops, and they say the more globular pieces, whiter and softer than the rest, are the marrow. The outer portion, however, like cortex is rougher and harder, blade-shaped, and of a pale yellowish-white color. If this kind of horn is easily crushed when you bite on it and is not tough like the horns, fraud is clearly indicated from its color and other distinctive signs, for it can be in fact the burned horn of some other animal, mixed with spices to make it palatable, or quenched whitehot in perfumed water.*

> *It is also false and deceitful for them to say that where unicorn's horn is lying and poison comes into its vicinity, the unicorn will sweat; it may well be that sometimes it does sweat, just like other solid bodies such as stone and glass on which vapours and moistures can outwardly freeze and then vanish again, without poison being any reason for that. For that occurs also with the stone called serpentine which they say shows where poison is present, but that is not so.*

> *Some people test for genuine natural unicorn horn as follows: Give some arsenic to a pair of doves, and give one of these a short drink of unicorn horn: if this dove remains alive, the horn is genuine and the other dove will die. Wealthy people may well use this test if they wish, since unicorn horn is so expensive, being sold weight for weight against gold, costing as much as a florin, a crown or a ducat per quintli (a weight varying from twenty-four to seventy-two pennyweights according to the district).*

> *Genuine unicorn is good against all poison, especially, so some say, the quality coming from the ocean isles. Experience proves that anyone having taken poison and becoming distended thereby, recovered good health on immediately taking a little unicorn horn. Thus one credible person told Mr. Gesner of having suspected taking poison in some cherries he ate, and feeling his stomach distended, which impelled him to take some unicorn horn marrow in wine, whereupon he recovered his health.*

90. Arms of the house of Baldung

This horn is useful and beneficial against epilepsy, pestilent fever, rabies, proliferation and infection of other animals and vermin, and against the worms within the body from which children faint.

Ancient physicians used their unicorn remedies against such ailments by making drinking mugs from the horn and letting their patients drink from them; nowadays such drinking vessels are unobtainable and the horn itself must be administered either alone or mixed with some other drug.

As to falling sickness or epilepsy, Mr. Gesner states he benefited one patient's health by making him a draft of unicorn to which he added amber, ivory scrapings, beaten gold, corals and other ingredients which he coarse-ground and put into a silken sachet, boiled down same in water containing red currants, cinnamon and other items, and then administered. Nor did he omit or neglect other remedies beside this.

Dr. Gesner's advice comes from the 1563 Zurich edition of his bestiary, and has been condensed here, spelled and phrased more in the modern manner for easier reading.

For centuries then the horn remained linked with antidotal or toxognostic power and supplied therapeutic medicaments. Not long after Hildegard, around the beginning of the thirteenth century, the first unicorn horns may have appeared in western Europe. In their straightness and with a characteristically natural spiral they corresponded to the preconceptions already in vogue about them: they had been so depicted in many an ancient psalter and gospel manuscript. To a medical world employing mysterious vegetable and animal extracts, portions of mummies, excrementa and the like, the unicorn came most opportunely. Whence it came was of course hard to verify: maybe from the East, like so many miraculous items? Whatever the facts, there it was, and as it grew horns, the rare animal itself must exist! Thus were the ancient accounts of its existence and the healing potency of its horn fortified with authority, and the diligent pursuits of theology and the sciences dependent thereon brought the ancient reports once more to the knowledge of a wider, scholarly world.

So now they scraped away carefully on the valuable horn, mixed the resultant powder into salves and potions, and occasionally cut off a ring to mix with other ingredients pounded together in the mortar. It was diligently prescribed against poisoning and epilepsy, just as the ancients had indicated. But now also it was prescribed against fevers of all kinds, plague, colic, and children's ailments so long as it was in stock. For a long time yet the horn, although a truly magnificent supply kept flowing from unknown sources, remained a rare and costly item and its use – as formerly in India – continued to be reserved for royalty and the rich. Thus there opened up opportunities for many a swindler who either supplied cow's hoofs as unicorn horn or produced fake horn, as Dr. Conrad Gesner angrily established when he reported, "In Venice there are several wicked scamps and vagabonds who mix a pulverized flint, lime or other stone with soap and make a paste therefrom which they sell as unicorn; for when they take a shaving off it and drop it into wine, it starts bubbling." [Ill. 154]

If the horn did not neutralize poison straight away, it at least indicated the danger, simply because the liquor began to effervesce. Cutlery with unicorn handles would sweat on contact with poisonous food. Such a defense was exceedingly important for temporal and spiritual rulers in the Renaissance who must have witnessed the death by poison of so many of their peers!

Even the proximity of the potent horn might have a beneficial effect, and so it became a favorite table decoration. Charles the Bold always had a piece of the horn ready on his dining board, and when this dreaded overlord visited Neuss (northern Rhineland) on one occasion, the townspeople knew of no better present than a unicorn beaker. Such effective vessels were long in demand, so that eventually they had to be counterfeited. Next to one another in the Hamburg Museum for Arts and Crafts lie a genuine beaker and one of ivory on which the spiral turns are artificially engraved. If need be, precious goblets were embellished with the unicorn, the entire animal at least figuratively enameled on the vessel itself or as a small sculpture on the lid. Thus it might also serve as a centerpiece on the table. In his autobiography Benevenuto Cellini tells of an order from the Pope (which however went to another goldsmith) to mount a unicorn's horn as a gift for Francis I of France. Unicorn settings were used for serving at table at the French court right up to the Revolution, but toward the end that may only have been a matter of form. [Ills. 140, 143, 146]

So potent a healing instrument naturally had a high market value, and there is plenty of evidence to that effect. In the first year of the reign of Queen Elizabeth I (1558) an inventory was taken at Windsor, in which a unicorn horn was recorded with a value of £10,000 (equivalent to say £50,000 or more, up to comparatively modern times). Her successor James I paid a similarly high amount for a horn (in which connection one British writer remarks that James was quite fittingly called "the wisest fool in Christendom"). To test the efficacy of his expensive medicine, James gave one of his servants a draft of poison with the unicorn powder and, when the man fell dead, declared he had been deceived, for clearly the horn was not genuine unicorn. Obviously the great royal houses owned such treasure but sometimes there was a certain amount of embarrassment. In 1588, the

Stockholm stockpile was exhausted, and King John III uregntly requested his son, King Sigismund of Poland, to supply him with a new horn. Perhaps it was easier to get one there nearer the East.

In Paris Ambroise Paré, experienced in many campaigns, physician to several kings of France, was a gifted pioneer of medicine, the greatest surgeon of the Renaissance and inventor of surgical instruments, of squint-correcting spectacles, and of an artificial hand. He mistrusted such medicaments as mummies and unicorn inherited from the Middle Ages but had to admit that the public demanded them. "Physicians are frequently compelled to prescribe unicorn or rather to allow patients to have them because they demand such remedies. For if it happened that a patient who had made such a request were to die without receiving what he wanted, the family would expel such physicians and disparage them in gossip as 'quite out of touch'." He is said to have spoken about this with a fellow court physician, saying that it was all a lot of humbug to dip unicorn horn into the cup from which the king was about to drink. His colleague replied that he was himself convinced of the inefficacy of the alleged antidote, but when Paré asked him to publish something attacking such foolishness, the other answered "I've got to look after myself! Anyone who writes against current public opinion is like an owl coming out into the daylight where all the other birds can swoop down and pluck him bare with their beaks."

Paré, who was then over seventy, decided therefore to campaign on his own against what he regarded as rank superstition, and in 1582 he published his discourse on *Mummies, Unicorns, Poisons and Plague*. In that book he reluctantly conceded that most probably unicorns did exist since the Bible says so; but the miraculous powers attributed to the horn were nonexistent and certainly were no cure for the plague. However, the horn might indirectly fortify the heart, since by virtue of its tellurian nature (alchemy still retained some hold, even on Paré!) it could have a contractive action closing the veins and arteries through which poison and noxious air would otherwise reach the heart. The Paris Faculty of Medicine vehemently counterattacked Paré's dangerous passion for innovation. When, however, they adduced the evidence of centuries in rebuttal, he replied "I would sooner be right by myself alone than wrong with the scholars or indeed with the rest of the world. For the grandeur of truth is so great that it surpasses all human wisdom."

The next light came from the north. During the Thirty Years War, a fine example occurred in Denmark of how unicorn frenzy could obsess entire families. When Professor Thomas Bartholin published his *De unicornu observationes novae* (New Notes on the Unicorn) in Padua in 1645, not only was his father Caspar one of the most cited authors with a book printed in

Copenhagen in 1628, but Thomas could point with satisfaction to the fact that his own son, another Caspar, was also occupied with the subject. Caspar the younger indeed published a new edition of Thomas's text in 1678, this time in Amsterdam. This book of thirty-seven chapters in its first edition must certainly be labeled as obsessed with the unicorn. The learned exposition starts off with a discussion whether there can be people with one or even two horns (although the alleged horns of Moses are explained in another special chapter along with the error in translation which was their real origin), and then runs through the whole of the animal kingdom down to the "fossil unicorn." Citations from an immense number of authors lead to the conclusion that the unicorn does exist though its horn did not possess the curative power ascribed to it. Foremost, however, it is now clearly stated what actually is sold by the apothecaries.

The relevant citation runs thus:

> *In the vicinity of our island of Greenland and other northerly isles an enormous marine creature is a frequent denizen, popularly known as the narwhal because it feeds on dead bodies (när in Danish). This creature resembling the whale in appearance and size has a tusk of unusual size growing from a gap in its front teeth, similar in length and strength to the horns we know so well . . . That tusk, however, is what so many have sold as unicorn and which is preserved in the treasuries of various rulers because of the singular appraisal of it as genuine unicorn. Such appraisal occurred easily in former times because of the scarcity of the tusk which only reached a foreign shore when the fish got stranded. Nowadays the increase of commerce with Greenland and Spitsbergen in particular has revealed the nature and frequent availability of the tusk. At all events, our merchants have filled whole cargo vessels with this alleged horn of recent years and would import it into Europe as genuine unicorn, had not experts torn away the mask and recognized the tusk as originating from the ocean.*

Now trade increased further not only to Europe but as far as Japan. Ten years after the appearance of Bartholin's book, the Merchants Guild of Copenhagen procured a certificate from Professor Ole Wurm on the commodity they were marketing as unicorn. If they had expected a kind of Public Relations Certificate for promoting sales, these merchants were disappointed by the learned expert. He confirmed that it was a narwhal's tusk. If those men of Copenhagen really did want to know exactly what they were dealing in, then they appear in a more honorable light than Bartholin imputed to them with his implication of conscious misleading of the public.

Be that as it may, at the beginning of the eighteenth century, a large quantity of "unicorn" specimens would have been foisted on the czar by a Greenland company had not his personal physician exposed the true nature of the goods in time and caused the deal to be cancelled.

The battle did not, of course, end right away with the Danish publications—not even for Denmark itself possibly. Some time in the 1660s Frederick III had the throne of the Danish monarchs constructed of narwhal tusks. Was that simply a matter of using a domestic product, or could it subconsciously conceal an idea of "Who knows what it's good for . . . ?"

People concerned in the trade evidently protected themselves. In 1663, Johann Joachim Becher, author of a famous medical treatise, energetically protested against the narwhal theory, so long as they did not "bring such horn from fishes in Novaya Zemlya and similar places, which so imitate our presumptive unicorn in form, appearance, strength and action that we cannot but conclude otherwise that all our known unicorn may be from those same fish." Meantime, however, the price of the horn had dropped considerably due to the importation of those huge shiploads. Guido Schönburger, to whom we owe the preceding quotation, has traced the evolution in prices for unicorn by the half ounce in Frankfurt apothecary shops thus: 1612 – 64 florins, 1626 – 32 fl., 1634 – 49 fl., 1643 – 32 fl., and 1669 – 4 fl.!

Pierre Pomet's *Histoire générale des drogues* (General History of Drugs) which appeared in Paris toward the end of the seventeenth century could only confirm the business of the narwhal, just as did the German edition under the more generally appropriate title *Der aufrichtige Materialist und Spezereihändler* (The Honest Grocer and Dry Goods Dealer). We may here point out that the word "Materialist" in the German title refers not to a materialistic philosopher, but to a *Materialwarenhändler* or wholesale druggist. Zedler's large encyclopedia *Grosses Universallexikon* in the eighth volume printed in 1734 doubts whether there really can be any quadrupedal equine unicorn in addition to the narwhal. The medicinal efficacy of narwhal tusk is equated to that of hartshorn and ivory but may nevertheless "be used reasonably in cases of emergency for children against erysipelas and measles, high fever, colic and other diseases (although in large doses than heretofore)" Next to that quotation is a prescription carefully coded for the use of apothecaries, covering the preparation of artificial unicorn "probably superior to real unicorn in potency . . ." Clearly the concern was to distinguish between genuine and ersatz unicorn rather than denying the existence of unicorn itself. [Ills. 129, 153]

91. From the Paris collection of Gobelins "Lady with Unicorn." Five members of the series are each supposed to represent one of the five senses. This illustrates the sense of sight

97. Lucas Kilian's sarcastic allegory on
◁ the Pope. Warrior bearing torch of
truth bars the way

98. A sixteenth-century relief from Castel
◁ Sant' Angelo

99. Piero della Francesca: Battista
Sforza's Triumph. Florence,
fifteenth century

101. Sixteenth-century fresco in Castel Sant' Angelo

102. Bernardo Luini: Unicorn with Procris, an association created by Renaissance imagination

127

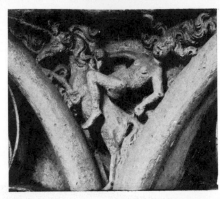

103. "Debauchery"?
A relief in the church
at Halle (Belgium). *ca.* 1400

105. Francois Clouet's painting of Diane
de Poitiers, sixteenth century. Note
unicorn on chairback in background

104. Chastity fighting Immodesty in a
fifteenth-century broadsheet

107. Knesebeck arms, Ratzeburg cathedral

106. Arms of Marx von Nussdorf, on tombstone in Laufen (Salzach)

108. Unicorn tympanum, Clermont-Ferrand

109. Seal from Schwabisch-Gmünd in Swabia, 1319

110. Bludenz bracteate, coin dated *ca.* 1260

111. Casement sketch by Hans Holbein
the Younger

112. Garden of Eden with unicorn (on the
right). Detail from the private altar
of Duke Albert V, Munich

114. Detail from painting of Paradise by
Lucas Cranach the Elder

113. Side of pew in Salzburg cathedral

115./116. The unicorn as symbol of Confirmation and Ordination on the baptismal font of the municipal church (formerly Church of Our Lady), Reutlingen. *ca.* 1500

118. Probably Low German aquaemanicle
(for warming of water)

10. On Helm and Scutcheon

The Lion and the Unicorn
Were fighting for the Crown;
The Lion chased the Unicorn
All around the town.
Some gave them white bread,
Some gave them brown,
Some gave them plum cake
And drummed them out of town.

Traditional English Nursery Rhyme

When knight errantry took shape and the Crusades accelerated the use of visible emblems rendered necessary by the form of battle, the Unicorn appeared eminently suitable for denoting a pious and courageous hero. **Endowed with tremendous strength and invincible courage, distinguished** as a symbol of the Savior by the virtues of meekness clad in mortal attire and of purity bowing only to the Virgin, it blazoned now on helm and scutcheon. In Wolfram von Eschenbach's *Parsival* (Sir Percevale of the Round Table, on whom also Wagner's *Parsifal* is modeled), Orgeluse laments over the defunct Zidegast, "A unicorn of loyalty was this man, the object of my desires. Humanity must lament the loss of this unicorn. Because of his purity he had to suffer death." The unicorn is mentioned as an armorial bearing in many of the early narratives and epics of chivalry.

In 1449 Jacques de Lalaing issued a challenge to knights on their way through Burgundy for a jubilee in Rome. Not yet thirty years old, his intention was to defeat at least thirty knights in the tournament before he reached that age. Near a tree dedicated to the memory of Charlemagne, he broke ground for a spring which he called *La fontaine des pleurs* ("The Fountain of Tears"). In a tent nearby he set up figures of a seated woman with a unicorn beneath an image of the Virgin Mary. On the first of each month for the space of a year he awaited the arrival of antagonists. Each adversary, mounted of course on horseback, had to fling his gauntlet at one of the three shields standing by the Virgin tent; each shield indicated a particular and different form of armed combat to which the opponent committed himself. A herald **stood ready to announce the acceptance of Sir Lalaing's challenge. Combat** then ensued according to a strictly established ritual, followed by a general banquet in the bishop's palace of Chalon-sur-Saone, while the accouterments used in the tourney were taken into a Lady Chapel. The proceedings were therefore ceremonial, gallant, and overtly without loss of blood. Chronicles relate that Lalaing vanquished twenty-two knights, an accomplishment which under all the stated conditions must have required more than the twelve assigned days unless he fought and feasted more than one antagonist on some days. He achieved still further deeds of valor but died at the age of thirty-two from gunshot in battle. This knight who under the aegis of the Virgin and unicorn had challenged all comers fell victim to the advent of technical warfare – a tragically ironic symbol not of triumphant but of decadent knighthood tottering to its fall.

Don Quixote, before being dubbed so oddly a knight errant, pondered over the names borne by some of his antecessors in the art – the knight of the griffin, of the phoenix, and "he of the unicorn" – but eventually adopted his squire's suggestion of "Knight of the Doleful Countenance" (or "of the Mournful Mayard").

In Germany the armorial significance of the unicorn developed most fully. In the Manesse manuscript of ballads, a silver-grey beast rampant on a blue ground is allotted to the minnesinger Dietmar of Aist, who came from Thürgau where many families are identified by this bearing. If we go into Franconia, Holstein, Swabia, or Austria, we find this handsome beast everywhere – on coats of arms and tombstones where its image provided attractive tasks for draftsmen and sculptors. It appeared in all sorts of manifestations. During the Renaissance passion for ornament the animal was delightfully embellished with two tails or sometimes even with a fishtail. Middle-class families began to adopt the sign, especially physicians or apothecaries who were acquainted with the assumed medicinal properties of the horn. From heraldry it passed logically into the sixteenth – and seventeenth-century symbology; it did service as a printers', publishers' and papermakers' stamp or colophon in book ornaments and vignettes. When the German poet Schiller was elevated to nobility, he adopted the unicorn as his heraldic beast, not, as one might suppose, because he was a physician nor even because it is a poetic beast, but because it had already long been used by his family, and indeed in a form similar to that used by a Tyrolese baronial family named Schiller von Herdern. [Ills. 106-108]

By far the best known unicorn in heraldry is part of the British coat of arms. When England and Scotland united at the beginning of the seventeenth century and James VI of Scotland became James I of the United Kingdom, a unicorn replaced one of the pair of lions supporting the shield. The menacing lion and antagonistic unicorn from Psalm 22 thus became fortuitously reunited in heraldry. The unicorn here came from the Scottish coat of arms, which still has a unicorn on each side as supporters. How and when the unicorn first reached Scotland is by no means satisfactorily explained though most probably this came about through some matrimonial connection with France indirectly through an English family. It was in use anyway at the beginning of the fifteenth century, when James I was reigning. Later in the same century James III had a gold coin struck bearing the beast and officially known as a unicorn. (A silver two-soldi piece minted in Ferrara in 1492 also bore the unicorn, taken in this case from the arms of the house of Este). [Ill. 89]

The heraldic beast was prolific in tapestries that embellished both tent and hall. The Borromeo princes in Italy ordered a set of tapestries for their Isola Bella castle on Lake Maggiore to portray all kinds of wild animals (by no means omitting their own armorial beast, the unicorn) disporting in jungles rather than in Paradise. From Italy the unicorn went to Austria through marriage of one of the Borromei into the family of an archbishop of Salzburg; thus it appears on every second pew in the cathedral, and the park of Hellbrunn's castle has two leaping seventeenth-century unicorns of elegant mien. [Ill. 113]

Despite the absence of family bond, clerics liked to choose the unicorn as their emblem because of its religious connotation, and in those cases where they owned landed estates they passed the same badge on to their city. That was the case with the city of Saverne, second residence of the bishop of Strassburg, and equally so for Amiens and Lyons. In the sixteenth century, the city of Hoorn in the Netherlands was persuaded by the diocesan bishop to adopt a pair of unicorns as supporters to its coat of arms. The design, which included a hunting horn (and sometimes also a cornucopia or horn of plenty), was joined in 1538 by a pair of unicorns; it is not easy to find a city like Hoorn where the unicorn turns up so ubiquitously – on the city hall, on the Weighbridge, on the orphanage, and on every public building.

Among German cities having the unicorn in their crest, Gmünd in Swabia is especially well known. Its oldest municipal seal bore the rampant beast from its origins in 1277. This unicorn, ready to attack, rears on cloven hoofs, its distinctive weapon pointing vigorously to the fore. The family of painter and engraver Hans Baldung, known as Grien or Grün (from his prolific use of green), probably derived its arms from this home town. The emblem can be seen beside the entrance to Lichtenthal priory church near Baden-Baden, on the tombstone of the painter's daughter-in-law, widow of Johann Baldung, mayor of Freiburg. [Ills. 90, 109]

The spiritual connection between gallant and seignorial man and the unicorn was expressed quite beautifully by the Holy Roman Emperor Charles V. When a courtier pointed out in the St. Denis treasury a "Hand of

Righteousness" carved from unicorn's horn, he is reputed to have said, "This may very well have been so pleasingly elaborated from such material, not because that substance is nicely clean, pure and clear, but rather because just as the unicorn counteracts all kinds of poison, so too may righteousness overcome and punish all vice and depravity."

During the age of chivalry the unicorn did not belie its traditional affinity for the ladies. It became a symbol of virginal purity for female saints from the Mother of God down. Also, on a Flemish tapestry in the Guildhall of Moravska Trebova (Trübau in Moravia), the Queen of Sheba appears with a unicorn as confirmation of her virtues in a favorite subject, her visit to Solomon; it stands with quiet conspicuity among her retinue. Progressively the unicorn became a symbol of womanly virtue in general. It became an attribute not only of female saints but also of ladies of distinction for whom the requirement of chastity may have been markedly bent. Diane de Poitiers, mistress of King Henry II of France, allowed François Clouet to paint her in the nude in the company of her child and the wetnurse; in the background is a piece of needlework embroidered with the unicorn. In contrast, the unicorn serves elsewhere as an emblem of chastity and simple virtue, especially in Italian paintings and miniatures purely in the abstract manner. Thus the image of purity associated with the Virgin appears in its original sense though now with somewhat more worldly connotation. [Ill. 105]

The finest example of this newer mundane concept is perhaps a medal of Cecilia Gonzaga, daughter of the marquis of Mantua, cast in 1447 by Antonio Pisano, otherwise known as Pisanello. This artist is credited with being the real father and at the same time the outstanding master of the art of medal engraving in the Italian Renaissance. The Gonzaga medal is regarded as the best of his creations. Cecilia herself is engraved on the obverse, and on the reverse we see a half-naked female figure, allegorically representing innocence as is confirmed by the huge male unicorn which lies at her feet, with his thick undulating pelt and horn thrusting straight forward. The damsel, with the calm quiet manner of one who knows she is mistress of the situation, is seen to be gripping the animal's horn at its point of emergence from the forehead. Over the inaccessible mountains hovers a crescent moon, the token of Artemis and a further symbol therefore of chastity. In this little masterpiece, archaic and Christian tradition merge harmoniously in a manner appropriate to the era. One of Pisanello's sketches in possession of the Uffizi gallery in Florence shows a still childish maiden in the role not of decoy but as protectress of the unicorn, which has sought refuge in her lap. Hounds and hunters respectfully retreat before her warning gesture. There is a concept diverging from most of the earlier portrayals; it is evident also in the repose of the Gonzaga medallion. [Ills. 49, 50]

One of Petrarch's poetical works was the effective impetus for the adaptation of this motif, namely the link of the unicorn with chastity, in the art of the Tuscan painters. The loss of his Laura was the motivation for the series of elegies which Petrarch entitled *Trionfi*. These are respectively the triumph of chastity over love, of death over chastity, of fame over death, of time over fame, and finally of eternity over time. These allegories have frequently been depicted, and where chastity appears victorious over love and prey to death, its chariot is drawn by unicorns. This concept was then applied to worldly ladies; princesses of the Tuscan dynasties are shown traveling by coach-and-unicorn through their territory. At a later date that motif was adopted by the tapestry industry of the Low Countries. Gorgeous collections of Gobelin tapestries with illustrations of Petrarch's *Triumphs* cover whole walls in museums in Vienna, London, and Madrid. [Ill. 99]

One German Protestant engraver of the Baroque period, Lukas Kilian, derisively applied this symbolism to the Pope, caricaturing him as drawn by a team of unicorns even as he believed the pontiff's possession of chastity doubtful indeed. Ironically such indirect or backhanded use of the unicorn demonstrates as dramatically as anything else the power of this image in its noblest role. [Ill. 97]

119. Albrecht Dürer's
Abduction on a unicorn

11. Wild Men and Women's Wiles

Hanging in a basket between heaven and earth is the Roman poet Vergil. He had an assignation with a young woman, possibly even an emperor's daughter according to some versions, who hauled him part way up a wall towards the window of her room. There he stays suspended in mid-air, a laughing-stock for the world at large, and when eventually the osiers give way, down he will fall through the bottom of the basket, only to realize then that the girl has literally dropped him. In a story of Indian origin, Aristotle apparently became so enamored of a woman of doubtful reputation that he willingly allowed her to ride him piggyback. Samson, the mighty slaughterer of Philistines, lay on Delilah's bosom and lost his strength when she cut his hair.

Such anecdotes of feminine cunning were readily told and illustrated during the Middle Ages and well into the Renaissance. The unicorn, too, was occasionally portrayed as a victim to feminine arts of enticement, thoroughly in harmony with the original gist of the story of its capture in the Hindu version. This occurred quite early, not as a travesty on the foregoing growth of the legend but concurrently with its development, and prior to its completion in the "Mystic Hunt." The unicorn in the maiden's lap and examples of other victims of women's wiles appear in a capital of a pillar in the church of St. Peter in Caen (Normandy) dating from the twelfth or thirteenth century. Another illustration is at Freiburg, the superbly dyed fourteenth-century "Malterer Tapestry" (named after the family who ordered this fine work of art). [Ills. 27, 77]

The ulterior erotic motif of the capture by the maiden is hinted at in the earliest *Physiologus* version. With the renewed circulation of this Hellenist book during the Middle Ages, that facet became clearer and clearer. This occurred almost simultaneously in the Near East and Europe, since *Physiologus* also experienced a renaissance in its oriental homeland, now under the stamp of Islam. As we saw, reciprocal influences between East and West certainly cannot be disregarded.

This variation on the enticement of the unicorn was a favorite with Arabian storytellers from the tenth century onward. The wild animal originally described as small as a kid or a lamb but untameable, leaps into the arms of the maiden as soon as he sees her "as though he were desirous of sucking her milk, this being his own sign of affection." Although he gets no milk, the act of suckling bemuses him as though with wines, so that the hunter can tether him. "Allah knows it best," is the phrase with which one Arabian author concludes the story – clearly not an expression of blind credulity.

No oriental assistance was needed for introducing erotic interpretation of the tale to the occident. In the oldest twelfth-century German edition of *Physiologus,* the unicorn dallies with the maid. The motif received preferential treatment and extension in France, where there was a particularly flourishing publication of bestiaries (treatises on the animal kingdom, modeled on *Physiologus* but constantly varying from it and supplementing it to a wider degree). Later, the tale penetrated into the minstrel lays of France and Germany. We have already hinted at the occasional recommendations that **the maiden displayed as a decoy should be naked, and as the beast comes** somewhat importunately to lick her breasts, she in turn "nuzzles it as she would a suitor surrendering himself to her"; we can have a certain modicum of understanding for the fact that, in one of the French versions, a lady – to her knight's dismay – shows not the slightest inclination to play the decoy for the beast. The enormity of that risk can be gathered from various descriptions in the French *Roman d'Alexandre* (Epic of Alexander) and Rudolf von Ems's *Weltchronik* (Chronicle of the Universe). According to these two works, the unicorn recognizes when the lady proffered to him is truly a virgin, and when she is not, he gores her. All this is occasionally accompanied by illustrations in which the religious significance of the unicorn legend also comes fully into its own.

A particularly striking example of the coexistence of sacred with profane ideas in the same period and in the same symbolic figure is the *Bestiaire d'Amour* (Bestiary of Love) compiled in the thirteenth century by Richard of Fournival (a village in Picardy). Although he was chancellor of the church in Amiens, he forbore from writing a devotional "divine" bestiary. His imaginary spokesman refers to the qualities of various animals in order to prove to his lady that she must listen to him with favor. In this, as the nineteenth-century French publisher of this work remarked, Richard exhibited a wide knowledge not only of the scientific literature of his day but also of the Codex of Courtship which had been modernized by romances of chivalry. Like the unicorn, the suitor is allured and stupefied by the maiden's fragrance. "Thus has Cupid taken revenge on me. In my arrogance I thought no woman however beautiful could ever inspire me with such violent love that I would crave to possess her. Cupid, that skillful hunter placed a crafty maiden in my path, and her sweetness dulled my senses. And now I am dying with love, a hopeless love with no prospect of favor." But

120.   Youthful savage, fifteenth century

the lady feels straightway warned by mention of the unicorn. Just as no armor can withstand its horn, so too, nothing in existence can more easily and more dangerously penetrate the hardest heart than gentle words. She must arm herself against them and he must strengthen other arguments with other animals. It is not surprising with such dialog that the publisher should feel reminded of eighteenth-century sweet talk.

A set of fourteenth-century articles of virtue belongs in this context. These include ivory caskets, jewel cases, and similar items manufactured on almost mass production lines in Paris. On the end of shorter panels of such caskets there is often a double decorated panel bearing, for example, a scene from *Tristram and Iseult;* the loving couple is sitting by the brook, while in the branches above them is the face of the jealous King Mark, reflected visibly also into the water so that Iseult, made aware of their peril, befools the king with innocent chatter. On the same casket-end, clearly conceived as an integral part of it, we see the familiar scene of the hunter slaying the unicorn in the maiden's lap. As on the silver miniature described earlier, the lady holds a garland or some similar object in her hand. The meaning of the juxtaposition of these two scenes is a matter of debate. Possibly it implies the antithesis of mundane and celestial love, of the secular and the clerical. Or, again, the virtuous maiden is possibly exhibited as a contrast to the iniquitous Iseult. Or it may even be a vulgar variant of the "women's wiles" and who then could we say is the victim? [Ill. 44]

While the unicorn again in the sense of the Hindu legend of the hermit Unicorn is trapped not by celestial but by absolutely sensuous love, the animal which has stood for chastity becomes simultaneously a symbol of concupiscence and, indeed, of lack of restraint. This is especially the interpretation of the Italian versions of *Physiologus;* the most prominent of their authors was Leonardo da Vinci. For him the unicorn represents *intemperanza* ("incontinence"), although he did not portray it thus in his art. Nevertheless the unicorn as a symbol of chastity in Italy immediately assumed just the opposite connotation. On a fresco which just misses being a sugary travesty in the Farnese Palace in Rome, Domenichino painted the great white beast as a horse with the addition of a goatee, resting in the lap of the gentle damsel and wholly as "he who surrenders to her" like a pining lover. Some portrayals in the Castel Sant' Angelo, on which the ladies taking part are shown nude and self-sacrificing, leave no doubt whatever that Zeus, Father of the Gods, after taking the form of bull and swan has here chosen a new form for approaching mortal woman – and that he had no reason to complain of any unwillingness in their surrender. The motto *Cedo alla purezza,* "I yield to purity," on a relief in the Castel Sant' Angelo library, also with lady and unicorn now in plain classical line, would not however be appropriate to

Leonardo da Vinci, sketch of a lady with a unicorn

those paintings. (Ills. 98, 103)

The game of the satyrs followed in Germany. The conflict between Chastity and Immodesty in that country is illustrated on tapestries and wood cuts for the delectation of a wider audience. These two antagonists ride against each other, Modesty on a handsome well-accoutered unicorn as though about to demonstrate the finest points of *haute ecole* horsemanship, while her unchaste adversary is mounted on a clumsy bear; their homeric dispute before the battle can be read on legends similar to our present-day comic strip baloons. [Ill. 104]

In southern Germany, the unicorn stepped into the indigenous myths. It became companion or antagonist to the savages. We encounter the savage or "wild man of the woods" (probably just a man of giant stature) occasionally as namesake for a hostelry or inn and in some southern German localities, **those wild companions, clad in animal pelts for winter would** come out of the forest to scare the ordinary people. Terror such as that aroused by Pan in ancient Hellas may have been the origin of those dwellers in the nordic forests. They probably represent the uncanniness and mystery which makes us whistle in the nocturnal wood. Richard Bernheimer, who has devoted a monograph to them, digs psychologically deeper:

122. Israhel van Meckenem, fifteenth-century joust between Man and Woman

> This strange relative of Homo sapiens, *a lively and sometimes pungent commentary on the bestial side of his nature, plays an outstandingly persistent, although on the whole subordinate, part in the art and literature of the Middle Ages . . . His presence is like the running commentary with which a man's half-conscious imagery accompanies his conscious ideals and aspirations: a reminder that there are basic and primitive impulses clamoring for satisfaction.*

The Wild Men dwelled in the forest, sometimes companionably, sometimes menacingly or inclined to pranks and monkey tricks (Rübezahl, the Silesian "Turnip Tail" demon, is assuredly related to them). They hunted all species of animals, cheerfully taking their loot back to a Wild Woman with child – an unabashed sideswipe at the homage of the Three Wise Men. Wild Man and Wild Woman blasphemously rode their mythical mounts – she on the unicorn, in a corral clearly reminiscent of the *Hortus conclusus*. The wild folk obviously fought the wild beasts and feared not even the unicorn. They were the only people able to break it in and even ride it. In that same period when the mystery of the religious hunt was developing, these ruffians with bow and arrow would mockingly force the unicorn toward one of the wenches of the woods. The forest queen would ride the unicorn bareback (both she and it) through the woods in the company of her riotous retinue carrying their plunder home on the tips of their spears. That scene is repro-

123. Albrecht Dürer, marginal sketch for Emperor Maximilian's prayer book

146

duced on a *Minnekastchen,* one of those wooden and leather caskets first so named in the age of Romanticism but obviously popular as keepsakes during the Gothic period. These boxes are frequently decorated with the unicorn portrayed in unmistakable scenes of lovemaking: the Wild Folk are to be seen riding on unicorns and other legendary beasts against the citadel of love, a combat said to have been retained as a popular sport in Swiss cities as late as the nineteenth century. [Ills. 7, 8, 52, 79, 120, 122]

Switzerland and the Upper Rhine between the Black Forest and the Vosges mountains were specially favored areas for those combined diversions and battles between Wild Folk and unicorns. Colorful tapestries depict them individually and collectively in the mysteriously intricate enchanted forest. Here again is the woman clasping the unicorn's weapon and thereby trapping it. And alone in the forest, by the stream, between birds and blossoms a pretty wench is sitting; as the legend on the picture tells us, she has dissipated her time in the world and must now live in wretchedness, but in compensation we see a darling dun-colored unicorn lying consolingly at her feet. The Virgin

124. Naked woman and middle-class woman with unicorns. Late fifteenth century pen-and-ink sketch

Mary has become a penitent Magdalen though not forsaken by all the world. This lovely work of art, a product of Strassburg, is in the possession of Basel Museum of History, which administers a collection of late Gothic figured tapestries, especially some with representations of the unicorn (where devotees can find several further unicorn portrayals). A parallel to the repentant forest wench is to be seen in the Minster at Constance. On one sidepiece of the pew is a nude Wild Woman with the unicorn, and on the other side she is shown alone entangled in the forest undergrowth. Even in **that satirical portrayal the spiritual meaning is plain; on one carving, the** human soul is in the thicket of sin, on the other, the redeemed soul is with its Savior. [Ills. 69, 70, 76, 78, 80]

A later neighbor of the Wild Folk is the muscular horseman abducting a **shrieking maiden in one of Dürer's engravings; he may be Pluto carrying off** Proserpina, or some other demoniac figure. The monstrous unicorn serving as his mount is also demoniac. In a period when it usually appears as a gentle domesticated creature on the gorgeous Gobelin tapestries, it is shown in this example with an originality and erotic force scarcely to be found anywhere else. The classical god, the savage pagan hunter, and the Wild Man of the German forest are coalesced into a single person for whom the mighty beast is appropriate, the result of which is altogether a thrilling image of the unicorn's elemental strength. [Ill. 119]

A smaller specimen yet by no means less powerful is one of the unicorns **sketched by Dürer in the margin of a prayer book for Emperor Maximilian.** This one also has a forward-curving horn. It stands erect almost on tiptoe, quiveringly tense with brute force, just on the point of retaliating against the attack of the angry crane. Some people have thought these beasts may be purely decorative and unrelated to the text. Erwin Panofsky, a scholar from Princeton University, past-master of iconology, observes on the contrary that they symbolize the words of Psalm 129 (130):6, 7, ". . .more than they that watch for the morning. Let Israel hope in the Lord." The crane here is the symbol of watchfulness. The unicorn represents the infernal region, darkness and night. [Ill. 123]

125. The unicorn—precious as the treasure shown

126. St. Justine by Moretto; she is receiving the unicorn for her virtuous defense of virginity

148

comment le corps · s · eftiene eft delaiffe au lieu de fon martire ·
et expofe au beftes et par la diuine puiffance preferue ·

12. 'My Sole Desire'

We may imagine that one of the works impelling Don Quixote on to his adventures was the ballad *de la dame a la lycorne et du biau chevalier au lyon,* "of the Lady with the Unicorn and the handsome Knight of the Lion," a favorite romance of chivalry which came into existence around the end of the thirteenth or beginning of the fourteenth century. The daughter of the king of Friesland was so beauteous and charming, so superlatively good, pure, and chaste, that the god of Love (whether Christ, who is mentioned a few lines before this passage, or the pagan Cupid we cannot decide) bestowed on her a unicorn, so that she might bear in perpetuity the appellation of "The White Lady, Ward of the Unicorn." The lady was married to a daring knight of high lineage, but that did not prevent her from bestowing her favors on the "biau chevalier." Among her many suitors, he possesses neither wealth nor outstanding education, but in honor of his lady, he sallies forth into the world bent on adventure and gains the title of Knight of the Lion (and with it also a lion in the flesh). When a lying informant brings the lady news of her knight's alleged death, she collapses and is abducted by some wicked man. Conversely somebody informs the Knight of the Lion that his lady is dead, whereupon he too first goes to pieces and then goes mad. Restored to sanity, he returns in order to ride (with the consent of his lady's husband) against the kidnapper's castle. He liberates his ladylove: on their beasts, the unicorn and the lion, they cross the moat surrounding the castle. The evil knight dies of rage, the handsome knight of the lion, preserving his platonic love (as is the style in bardic ballads), rides forth to fresh adventures. The unicorn is put to work only this once.

Occasionally people have believed this ballad was the pattern for the set of tapestries that, under the designation of "The Lady of the Unicorn," is the pride of the Cluny Museum in Paris. But that opinion does not stand up to examination of the tapestries and the ballad. Beyond the consonance of the names and the presence of the two heraldic beasts on the tapestries, the two works of art are linked only by the allegoric atmosphere of an aristocratic and knightly court (with an interval of almost two centuries between their respective geneses). [Ills. 91-96]

Whoever sets foot in the huge circular hall which the Cluny Museum has built for its most famous treasure will find it difficult to escape the spell

26a. Animals on guard over corpse of Stephen the Martyr

of what is deemed the finest set of medieval tapestries. The architect who designed the hall now housing them may not have modeled it on a chapel but rather on a tent such as those favored by the Burgundian lords for their feasts, jousts, and campaigns. But the romance of the name "Lady with the Unicorn" and the breath of poesy spun around the series by writers of note create an atmosphere of a reverence which rather than being intrinsic to the original production of the Gobelins is something added with the passing of time. Even one armed with skepticism and cold reason may succumb in the long run to the lyric charm which emanates not from the exhibition and history of these works of art but from their very essence.

These six tapestries vary in length from 9'6" to 15'3" and in height from 10'0" to 12'6". In each of them the eye is immediately struck by the soft red background, flower-studded in the floriate style popular in French and Flemish fabrics at the beginning of the Renaissance, and the mass of blossoms is alive with a multitude of small animals, hares, sheep, dogs, and apes; nor are foxes and other predators lacking, and both peaceful and menacing species of birds are included as well. Each design comprises a deeply dyed insular oval also strewn with flowers and populated with animal figures. Trees and shrubs abound here, ilex, oak, orange, and pine. In the middle of the island on each hanging stands a lady in court dress, always sumptuous and different in each picture, accompanied by a smaller maid or female friend (except in two of the six pictures) also in eyeworthy, gorgeous attire.

On all six pieces we see the two ancient mythical and heraldic rivals and companions, the lion and the unicorn, to the right and left of the human figures on the island. They carry standards always bearing the same arms, namely three white half-moons on a blue riband across a rose-colored field. In one case the lady herself is carrying the banner. Of the two large animals, the unicorn is the one which twice opens direct relation with the lady. On one of the designs, where the "servant-girl" is missing, it rests with its forefeet in the lap of the seated lady, looking into a mirror she is holding in front of its face. The scene is reminiscent, although in secular courtly context, of that capture of the unicorn by the virgin described in *Physiologus* and so often represented in artwork, while the mirror too is a Marian symbol. On the second tapestry lacking the smaller female figure, the lady is standing banner in hand and gripping the horn with that possessive or loving contact which tames the beast. On yet another the lady is seen playing a melodeon (her female companion is working the bellows) yet again adorned with statuettes of lion and unicorn; the companion also offers her mistress a bunch of flowers, or on another of the tapestries, some fruit.

The scene changes on the last of these hangings. A stately gold and azure tent is set up on the island and in front of it the lady is selecting jewelry and ornaments from a casket handed to her by the other woman. On the frieze of the tent like a dedicatory motto are the words A MON SEUL DESIR V (the final letter, which is a source of puzzlement, is also read as a J). Also on the tapestry where the lady is taking fruit from a dish, a graceful animal is sitting on the red background close to her head – definitely a unicorn colt. Its horn has not yet sprouted (and most probably these animals cannot be born complete with horn). Hanging in the hall near these tapestries is a "genuine" unicorn shaft impressive with its length of eight feet or more. This may be the one that was once part of the royal treasure at St. Denis.

It rapidly becomes evident that these designs are not illustrations to some romance but are allegorical in character. What they are supposed to mean has, however, caused much cogitation by scientific authorities. The increasingly prevalent theory is that these may be representation of the five senses (the mirror for sight; the melodeon for hearing; the flowers for smell; the fruits for taste, and the contact with the horn for touch). This was advanced by a British art historian in 1921 and has meantime been accepted also by the curators of the Cluny Museum. The sixth hanging with tent and motto might then be so to speak a dedicatory supplement, even though the inscription contains something still to be deciphered.

To get at some interpretation, it was and is highly desirable to establish something cogent regarding who commissioned the work and what was the object of the set. On the first point at least progress was made quite early since the bearings with the three crescent moons were identifiable. They have no connection with the orient as suggested by the romantic legend purporting that the customer was a certain Turkish Prince Zizim (who is historically known to have been a fugitive in France toward the end of the **fifteenth century). The arms are now attributed to the Le Viste family of craftsmen who acquired wealth, influence, and (not without opposition)** noble rank in Lyons. Around the turn of the century, the head of the family was living in Paris, occupied with financial affairs, but possessed some property in Burgundy. If the unicorn and lion pair could have been chosen in consideration of his established heraldic preference, the unicorn might be additionally explained by a play upon words; according to this version it **was intended to stand for *vitesse* (speed), certainly as a play on the name** *Le Viste*. Records have established that the family had other unicorn tapestries in its possession but these have not survived.

The hangings in the Cluny collection might for instance have been manufactured for a wedding in that house. No later than 1513 a certain Claudi a Le Viste contracted a second marriage with one Jean de Chabannes. His first name might explain the last letter on the inscription, if we are to read it as a J. The bridegroom, though short of stature, was courageous and bore the nickname "Lion Cub," thus adding extra meaning to the lion on the tapestries. The unicorn is then thought to stand for the Le Viste family, not precisely for the lady, who as a widow was no longer entitled to the symbol of virginity. (Were people, however, really so fastidious and unready to take the unicorn also more commonly as a symbol for virtue?) This explanation of the origin of the tapestries has not been confirmed, and that final single letter could in any case also be some arbitrary mark for the production of typographic symmetry, so that the inscription could signify the dedication *A mon seul désir,* "To my sole desire."

Equally obscure is the question of exactly where those magnificent hangings were produced. On that point, suggestions have covered all the famous localities of the French and Low Countries' carpet industry: Aubusson, Tournai, Bruges, and recently Brussels in particular, to say nothing of itinerant warp setters from the Loire. Nobody knows, but it is unanimously agreed that the designer certainly was an unknown master craftsman of the French art. Indeed, what was produced in this case goes far beyond a magnificent piece of handicraft (so far as such differentiation is permissible for that period in general). The composition—the lady always at the center, the distribution of the decorative elements, the noble flow of the lines—demonstrates its quality quite apart from the wealth of invention (which certainly to some extent touches on tradition and routine) and from the treatment of dyes and materials. Only the unicorn on the piece now designated as "Sense of Hearing" looks remarkably clumsy and badly drawn, as though here some other hand had interfered.

Now let us take a short glance sideways at an item which is close to our subject in more sense than one. Also hanging there in the Cluny Museum is a sequence of tapestries practically 148 feet long overall, portraying the life, death, and miracle of St. Stephen. One of these hangings shows the martyr lying dead in the forest. The assassins who have stoned him to death are making their escape (Saulus, who was minding the raiment, belongs in their company). Near the lonely corpse, various animals are keeping watch: the stag, lion, porcupine, and ape, and with them the unicorn with the tip of his weapon pointing upward where the angels are in the act of carrying Stephen's soul up to heaven. Although in this case the flower-studded background has not been used, having been replaced by a completely executed horticultural landscape, the design prevents several similarities with the Lady and Unicorn tapestries. The unicorn itself in its unsullied grace reminds us of the dedicatory tapestry *A mon seul désir.*

These tapestries of St. Stephen were ordered by the bishop of Auxerre for his church around the year 1500. That bishop, Jean Baillet by name, was a brother-in-law of Aubert Le Viste, the head of the Le Viste family and counselor and comptroller to Charles the Bold. It is easy to imagine that these relatives had done business with the same tapestry manufacturers and to appreciate the remarkable destiny which has brought both those works of art together on adjacent walls after the passing of centuries.

Something further has to be said about the Le Viste tapestries. Some years ago a fresh light was stimulatingly shed on everything concerned with their origin, meaning, and purpose. Maria Lanckorońska expounded and exhaustively substantiated her thesis that the "Lady with the Unicorn" can be identified with none other than Margaret of York, third spouse of Charles the Bold of Burgundy. Aubert Le Viste as his banker and confidant would have ordered this magnificent gift to be made for the new consort (thus allowing us credibly to interpret the initials on either side of the motto *A mon seul désir* as A and V for Aubert Le Viste.) Clearly, since such a commission would have taken many years to complete, the tapestries may not have been finished early enough for the ceremony and meantime with the death of the duke the politically favorable situation changed so that the tapestries would therefore have remained in the possession of the Le Viste family.

A spirited unicorn did make its entrance at the wedding in July 1468 of Charles and Margaret in Bruges. A lavish feast was spread in a great hall hurriedly erected on the tennis court and as interludes between the courses many splendid displays were presented, *tableaux vivants* and scenes in effigy as well as massive parades and processions. Olivier de la Marche, captain of the ducal guard, has described this festivity in his memoirs of the court of Burgundy:

> *First there entered the hall a unicorn large as a horse and fully caparisoned in a silken cloth bearing the arms of England painted thereon. Seated on the beast was a very fine painted leopard almost true to life; in one forepaw it carried a huge banner of England and in the other a beautifully fabricated marguerite. Now the unicorn having made its way around the tables to the sound of clarions, was led in front of my master the Duke, and one of the ducal stewards thereupon plucked the blossom from the leopard's claw and kneeling addressed the Duke, "Most mighty, noble and conquering Prince, my honored and worshipful Lord and Sovereign! The proud and fear-inspiring leopard of England visiting this honorable assemblage presents for the delight of Your noble self, Your allies, realms and subjects, to You in person a Marguerite (Margeret) of noble birth." Thus did my master receive the noble Margaret, and the unicorn returned thither whence he had come.*

The flower is clearly the symbol of the new duchess and the leopard is her heraldic beast. The unicorn, however, does not represent England (into whose coat of arms it had not at that time yet been incorporated) but stands for the bride's virtues. It was, anyway, greatly favored at the Burgundian court, although its symbolic meaning exerted no lasting effect. Two of the bishops there present were illegitimate sons of deceased dukes.

Maria Lanckorońska has substantially more than the above narrative to offer in support of her theory. One of the animals seated right by the lady's feet is a *genette* ("civet cat") among the *plantae* ("shrubs"), forming thus a rebus on *Plantagenet,* the house from which Margaret was descended, and, just like the marguerites themselves, symbolic in this case of her name. The garland which the lady is plaiting consists of white and red roses, tokens of the rival houses of York and Lancaster (with which the latter Charles was related) now united by this marriage. The leopard with its collar of **marguerites is the bride's heraldic beast and also came to the ceremony.** And besides many other details, the "Lady with the Unicorn" has not only the same tall, slender figure as Margaret but also resembles her in face and features.

127. Linsey-woolsey hanging with story of Pyramus and Thisbe

But now we onlookers are brought to a sudden halt. The ladies on the individual tapestries bear no resemblance to one another, so how should they be presumed to resemble still a seventh? The radiant young beauty on the hanging we label "Taste" is so little like the mournful-looking exemplar of "Sight" that the different coiffure and even a suspicion of distortion on the part of designers or weavers scarcely admit any idea of there ever having been any likeness among the various figures. Was it technically possible at that time to produce true-to-life portraits in tapestry and was it even contemplated in this case? Some of the evidential detail is also questionable. The lady is not, in fact, making a garland of roses (that is to say the emblems of the houses of York and Lancaster) but of pinks or carnations. And many tapestries of the period have marguerites, as well as other flowers, in their decoration. A more intrinsic basis of argument seems of greater importance than stylistic details. Can it be seriously imagined that a man, however newly rich he may be, who wanted to flatter his liege lord the powerful Duke of Burgundy, would have had the impudence to have his own armorial bearings and them alone portrayed on the intended gift sequence and even make the princess herself the bearer of those tokens in her own hand? However carefully Maria Lanckorońska has constructed the scientific foundation of her interesting hypothesis, and however attractive it might be to imagine the "Lady with the Unicorn" as the spouse of one of the most brilliant men of his time (and she herself also a woman of consequence), we cannot legitimately ratify the idea. Though her image does not get far on a

156

128. The expulsion of the serpents

historical basis, it certainly does not lose anything in lyrical charm, even though we grant that it really is not a matter of "The Lady with the Unicorn" but of "Ladies with Lions and Unicorns."

So bold and carefully concocted a thesis as Maria Lanckorońska's contains its attraction for the spectator and its due of stimulus for science, even though one skeptically opposes its outcome in the final analysis. Even the curator of the Cluny Museum, Francis Salet, has expressly acknowledged the scientific thoroughness of the idea. But he quite decidedly rejects any identity between the Unicorn Lady and Margaret of York. With unemotional scholarliness he declines all romanticism regarding the "Lady with the Unicorn." For him, the whole sequence of tapestries is of a purely heraldic nature, intended to introduce extravagantly the coat of arms of a parvenu family, with a motto *A mon seul désir,* the meaning of which still requires elucidation. "And everything else is fantasy." And he is quite right, although that "everything else" is in part great literature and can still tempt poetic natures looking for secrets behind a work of art. Since its rediscovery, this tapestry has been enveloped in an aura of romance. Through marriage in mid-seventeenth century, it passed to the castle of Boussac in central France (in the Department of Creuse) and later was sold with the whole of the contents of the castle to the city. It lay rolled up in a corner of the city hall, gnawed by rats and mildewed by damp, offering an example of the neglect to which items of intangible value can be subject. Discovered by a writer (Prosper Mérimée, Inspector of Fine Arts), enthusiastically brought before the public by an authoress (George Sand in her novel *Jeanne* and in an essay for *L'Illustration,* 1847), these hangings frequently appealed to the creative spirit and not only to scientific judgment. Outstanding among champions of their beauty were Marcel Proust and Rainer Maria Rilke, who was deeply impressed by the tapestries during his sojourn in Paris as secretary to Rodin. In Rilke's novel *Malte Laurids Brigge* (titled in English as *Journal of My Other Self*), Malte pictures himself conducting his beloved Abelone along the row of tapestries. And he too sees (and so we must concede that much also to Maria Lanckorońska) "always one figure, one woman in different garb yet ever her unchanging self." The last one he looks at is the hanging now labeled "Sight" on which the lady holds a mirror up to the unicorn's face. The image reappears in the fourth poem of Part Two of the *Sonnets to Orpheus.* This is the profoundest poetic homage to the unicorn, which is seen here as a pure production of the human soul, freed from all the dross of a curious and frequently chaotic history. The intention is, as Rilke wrote on June 1, 1923, to Countess Sizzo, "all love to the unauthenticated and intangible, all credence in the value and authenticity of what our mind has through the ages created from itself and placed on a pedestal." If expressly in this place "no parallel with Christ is implied," Rilke has included the Christian relevance of the unicorn elsewhere in his writings. In his *Life of the Virgin Mary*, in the Annunciation poem, he says of the Virgin, a doe had "so merged into her purity that the unicorn engendered in her absolutely without copulation the beast of light alone, the perfect creature." "Like a steeple on the moon," the horn stands erect as the animal visits the praying hermit. Once more the myth has come into its own.

29. Miscellaneous types of unicorn, including a two-horned mutant, from Pomet's *Pharmaceutics*, seventeenth century

13. Captured Yet Free

New York, modern as it is, possesses a Romanesque cloister. It stands on Manhattan in the seclusion of a woodland park overlooking the Hudson. How, we ask, can a cloister so ancient be in such a setting? Of course it has been synthetically reconstructed. Reading how oil-king Rockefeller bought up the ruins of European abbeys and priories, numbering the stones serially for rebuilding in the New World, the European out of intellectual snobbery will smile haughtily at such parvenu outvying of his culture. But his superiority may subside if he actually visits the spot. "The Cloisters" are intended for the exhibition in a tasteful setting of the medieval European art treasures which Rockefeller had already presented to the Metropolitan Museum. Here too some prejudice may resist an artificial revival of the past. And yet whoever sees the range of ethnic groups represented in the crowds wending their way through the halls, passages, and gardens to see masterpieces from Italy, France, Spain, and Germany, immersing themselves in the atmosphere there, receives a strong impression of the American will not only to take over its inheritance materially but to absorb it internally, with utmost sincerity, as well.

The masterpiece in this edifice is a set of hangings which makes the Metropolitan rival to the Cluny Museum of Paris in possession of the loveliest medieval hangings and, in particular, the most beautiful unicorn tapestries. Hardly can they be said to be less representative; they are incomparably more dramatic. They relate a story, the hunting of the unicorn, but mundane and ecclesiastical motifs from the symbolic history of the unicorn merge, once more, in these works. [Ills. 130-135.]

On the first of seven tapestries a company of richly clad young people is setting out for the chase accompanied by hounds and huntsmen. A scout sent out ahead has obviously already spotted the quarry and is beckoning from the forest. The next hanging shows the beast. Animals are assembled around an artistically sculptured Renaissance well, wild animals as well as tame, lion and deer, wolf and hare, and a goldfinch and a pheasant are roosting on the wellhead. Amidst them all we see the white unicorn. He is kneeling on his forelegs, doing what *Physiologus* reports him to have done in the oasis, what John of Hesse saw by the river Mara, namely dipping his horn into the water and purging it of poison. Round about in the copse, the now very augmented hunting party is watching the unusual scene, pointing at the white beast, and discussing the matter in groups. But amazement quells the hunting fever only for a short while. Two hangings follow, showing the encircled unicorn in the struggle. Attacked from all sides with spears, pursued by hounds, it seeks salvation by leaping across the brook, kicking out backward, and spearing a mongrel dog in front of him.

On the fifth tapestry, of which we have unfortunately only two fragments (logical arrangement in the sequence of action may therefore be a little uncertain), the animal under pursuit is in a fenced-in garden. This is that *Hortus conclusus* in which we found the Virgin Mary and her child. Like the archangel Gabriel, a huntsman blows his horn. The mystic unicorn hunt, a favorite tale in Germany at that time, here becomes a section of a temporal royal hunt. Does the success of the hunt have to be preceded here also by the taming by a woman? A lady is there, but not *the* lady. She must be a maid-servant, who with raised hand and a suspicious look, appears to be repelling the hunters. Like the hunters, the lady who supposedly should tame the unicorn is not to be seen on the fragment. We can see only a sleeve and the fingers of a slender hand, gently approaching the unicorn's mane. But in this case, the maiden's hand brings no rescue. The hunt progresses unrelentingly.

So much has to be told that two scenes are shown together on the sixth tapestry. Again surrounded, harried by a pack of hounds, hit by two spears in neck and chest, the noble beast collapses. With the oaken shaft in its mortal wound, the animal is slung over a horse's shoulder and conveyed to a princely pair who proceed with a curious crowd through the gate of a much-turreted city. The drama is ended. Yet not so! The unicorn is again visible on a seventh hanging, bleeding from his wounds but alive, in a timbered corral tethered to a tree by a golden chain, alone on a flower-studded carpet. Unmistakably, the christological meaning of the unicorn is taken up here with a new twist. The Lord is risen, but there is no joy of Easter. A deep melancholy pervades the image of the beautiful animal, so much more tender than on the other hangings and so absolutely alone, a **symbol of wounded and shackled nobility in an unappreciative world.**

Life and death adjoin each other in the sign of the unicorn, which since antiquity is the promise of health but also the end of life. The Cleveland **Museum of Art possesses a set of Gobelins, formerly in the French chateau** de Chaumont (Loire-et-Cher). It is described as *Allegorie de l'ephemere* (Allegory of the Ephemeris), and one of the four tapestries has the theme "Youth and **Age." These two stages of life are separated by a stockade. On the left** Youth is leading its happy, carefree life; on the right an old man is being brutally cudgeled by a younger one. Near this cruel scene, a white unicorn **crouches as though quite uninterested—one must indeed take it as a symbol** of Death just as in those representations of the man in the well.

As with those found in the Cluny, the place of origin of this great series of unicorn tapestries in the Cloisters cannot be determined. The reason **for their manufacture is, however, known with fair certainty. They— or more accurately, the second to sixth tapestries—were a gift for** the wedding of Anne of Brittany to Louis XII of France on January 8, 1499. This Anne is a remarkable example of how in her day princesses were treated as spineless sacrifices of princely power politics. She was twelve years old when in 1488 her father's death made her heiress to the duchy of Brittany and therefore a very desirable match. Ought the duchy be merged into the growing centralized government of France or should it seek association with some other power? The young princess' advisers decided to betroth her with Maximilian of Austria, already widowed after his marriage to Mary of Burgundy, and arranged the marriage by proxy. Thus the future German emperor hoped to gain a new foothold in the West, behind the back of France, instead of the shaky state of affairs in the Low Countries. His own daughter Margaret was betrothed to the young king Charles VIII of France and was already staying at his court in training for her future duties. But abruptly this so carefully prepared scheme was upset. Margaret was sent packing back home and Anne compelled by force of arms to wed the French king instead of Maximilian. Her new husband was in such a poor state of health that the marriage contract provided that in the event of his death, the young wife must straightaway wed his successor to the throne of France. Eight years after the marriage, that event occurred in 1498. The house of Valois became extinct with the death of Charles VIII, and his successor from the house of Orleans took the title of Louis XII. To bind Brittany to the State, he had to get a divorce in order to marry the young widow Anne in accordance with the contract. Apparently he was not at all loth to comply with that condition. Thus Anne became Queen of France for the second time, and for this second marriage the unicorn hunt tapestries were made to celebrate a widow's wedding.

The letters which appear in various places on the tapestries, an A and specular E, are read as the initial and final of the name Anne. They are joined by a knotted cord. Anne was by tradition a devotee of St. Francis, and the Franciscans girded their robe with such a cord. Anne founded an order of nobility for ladies to which she gave the title *Dames de la Cordelière* ("Ladies of the Knotted Cord"). The lone unicorn on the final hanging is indicative of Anne's second marriage. The multifaceted use of the unicorn as a symbol is not excessive if one assumes that it does not solely apply to the Resurrected; indeed, mundane and religious meanings co-exist. Fenced in and tethered, it indicates the accomplished bond of matrimony, the pomegranate tree under which it reclines, or more precisely the fruit of that tree, is in itself an ancient fertility symbol.

This seventh tapestry stands apart in style from the series as a whole; that applies in some measure also to the first of these hangings. It is therefore assumed that only the five in the middle, which portray the actual hunting of the unicorn, were manufactured to begin with, the first and the last being later additions. This may have been the case soon or somewhat later, for instance, when Anne's daughter by this second marriage wedded King **Francis I. However, the monogram FR (could that be Franciscus Rex?)**, which might indicate this interpretation, appears on a portion of the original **set, while Anne's initials are, on the other hand, embodied in the first and last tapestries. The difference in style does not necessarily indicate any time interval: the work might have been commissioned from another factory, or perhaps the design arranged for the set was felt to be too harsh and the manifold symbolism of the living, resuscitated unicorn was gladly accepted as an excellent option. This unicorn portrayal with its flower-carpeted background differs in design and emotional content from all the other components of the set, even from the first one, which is comparatively conventional and inflexible in its effect.**

The whole of this Cloisters series underwent a fate similar to that of the Cluny collection. It came apparently early into the possession of the family **of La Rochefoucauld and was included in the inventory for the year 1728** of their castle of Verteuil in the southwest of France. During the French Revolution, the tapestries were confiscated and indeed mutilated wherever they contained any tokens of royalty. Occasionally, it is said, they were used for carrying potatoes and concealing them during shortages. Later still, the tapestries came once more into the hands of the La Rochefoucaulds and returned to Verteuil, their quality apparently not being fully discerned and even disregarded in the older unicorn literature. Then J. D. Rockefeller purchased them in the 1920s and donated them to the Metropolitan Museum of Art in 1937. And since then America has made the unicorn its own not only in a superficial sense.

The lone unicorn in the Cloisters is a solitary pinnacle of Art. It is now **being gradually rediscovered even in Europe. Poets will seize upon it as they did the Parisian "Lady with the Unicorn." Anne Morrow Lindbergh dedicated a song of praise to the noble unicorn that has travelled, in many ways, so far from eastern origins. For her, it is "in captivity, yet free."**

132. The unicorn at the spring

133. The unicorn takes to flight

**Five Gobelins from the "Unicorn Hunt"
Series, circa 1500**
Figure 130 shows the last of the series; the
one existing in fragmentary form is not
reproduced here

131. The start of the hunt

134. The battling unicorn

135. The unicorn smitten in the neck and
brought dead into the castle

136. Sixteenth-century symbolism of alchemy; the stag as Soul, the unicorn as Spirit, the countryside as Substance of Mankind

137. Adam in the Garden of Eden, Marble intarsia, sixteenth century, Sienna

138. Sketch (tapestry cartoon?) for Charles
▷ de Bourbon, Cardinal Archbishop of Lyons, *ca.* 1500

139. Wellhead from Neuburg on the Danube, *ca.* 1530

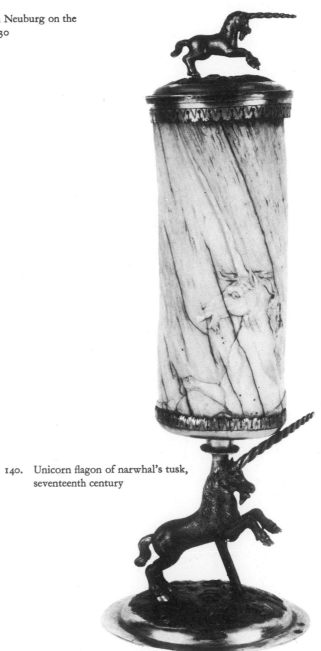

140. Unicorn flagon of narwhal's tusk, seventeenth century

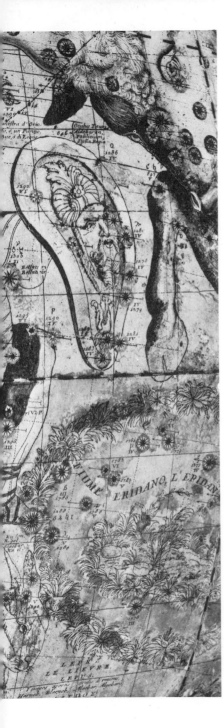

141. Detail of celestial sphere of
◁ eighteenth century

142. Elieser Susmann's ceiling of Horb
▽ synagogue (Detail)

143. Burgundian ornate flagon, fifteenth
◁   century

144. Unicorn shaft used as apothecary's
▷   sign in Rottenbuch, *ca.* 1750

145. Mortar with apothecary's crest,
▷   Frankfurt

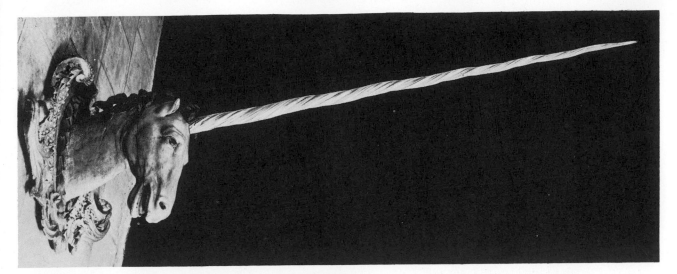

146. Unicorn amulet made from segment
  ▷ of narwhal tusk, *ca.* 1600. Note
     signs of scraping

147. Ernst Fuchs, *The Begetting of the*
◁ *Unicorn* and *The Unicorn's Triumph*

148. The artist and the unicorn by Ernst
· Fuchs

149. Rosita Salem's "magic realism"
▷ treatment of the unicorn shows the
horn as a primitive force

176

150. Gustave Moreau, *Ladies and Unicorns*,
     nineteenth century

151. Triumph of Innocence. Stained glass
     window from Rouen, 1515

152. Jean Duvet, King pursued by unicorn: sixteenth-century copperplate engraving

14. The Living Unicorn

It could have happened this way: thousands of years ago some Persian hunter saw an ibex in profile against the open sky in the mountain uplands and told everyone he had seen a unicorn. Or the same could have happened with an Arab or some other native of Africa at the sight of a gazelle. And thus we can have a perfectly "natural" explanation of how the unicorn myth began. For centuries people sought the original of the animal and not simply what looked like a unicorn when seen in profile. Travelers other than adventurers reported from Asia and Africa the existence of unicorns, though more frequently from hearsay than personal observation. Well into the nineteenth century explorers and hunters lay in ambush for the legendary beast; no less eagerly did their twentieth century successors await the yeti, the abominable snowman in the Himalayas. Acknowledged scholars such as Edward Rüppell, to whom the Senckenberg Institute in Frankfurt owes a considerable portion of its African collections, have declared it probable, **possible, and conceivable that the unicorn existed. It has been sought in** the gorges of the Ethiopian mountains where Cosmas the "Indian sailor" had said it lived, and in the rock caverns of South Africa where paintings **presumably of unicorns seen by earlier cavemen had been found. Ernst** Fuhrmann, another twentieth-century archaeologist as learned as he was imaginative, stated he was convinced there have been unicorns in Europe and Asia, although unfortunately he had not produced any evidence to support his conviction. Perhaps he was thinking of the elasmotherium, that **Siberian beast we have encountered through "eyewitnesses."**

But what, we may ask, has all that to do with the "honest-to-goodness" unicorn? Even if early naturalistic experiences led to a chain of associations which kept the animal alive, the unicorn has strayed far from its origins. Not only has its form and figure altered in many ways, not only has it served as a symbol for manifold and contradictory concepts; it also gained existence from and unto itself, from a new source after the naturalistic beginning. The unicorn is a creation of the human mind and it is as real as any such creations **are. The unicorn is as unreal or as real as a poem or a dream. Thus it has existed in various periods, various conceptions, and various degrees of** intensity. Notably enough, in this sense, it exists today in the age of a new enlightenment.

For the special case of the unicorn myth we might well repeat what the **Romantic scholar and poet Schlegal exclaimed in a** *Discourse on Mythology:* "If only the treasures of the Orient were as accessible to us as those of antiquity!" What is known of the unicorn from Asia is so fragmentary that no precise idea of its earliest mythological significance is possible. Certainly the animal, previously credited in China with annunciatory functions (what a prototheme for the "mystic hunt" in the German Middle Ages!) is **different from the supplier of antidote and astragali or anklebones** which the Greeks regarded so prosaically. India was the original home of the ideas from which the unicorn eventually came into existence, but whether ancient India knew anything of a unicorn in our occidental sense beside the rhinoceros with its figurative meaning of mildness and good temper is most doubtful. In the Near East, disregarding premature and undocumented findings, the essential unicorn evolved only contemporaneously with the Middle Ages in Europe (and the influence of early Christian conceptions such as *Physiologus* is plain). Even though oriental imagination pursued its own creative course, the traditions of several cultures underwent a remarkable fusion: the unicorn victoriously chases the elephant as in the tales of the *Arabian Nights' Entertainments,* it fights knights and heroes, and it is decoyed by the maiden as in the Christian *Physiologus.*

Through Christianity the unicorn infiltrates the region of myth. No longer is it important whether one believes in the physical existence of the unicorn, although that had long been the case. The important thing is what inner power it has. It becomes and remains a symbol, even though a homelier naiveté may occasionally have blurred the boundary between "that connotes . . ." and "that is . . ." Even where this is not so, the symbol acquires reality as an utterance from the human soul, as a fulfillment of some spiritual need, and as a filling of space which ought not to be left empty. "Symbolism is the commonest way for creativity to achieve reality" in the words of Dagobert Frey. A symbol has a character which is super-**personal, binding, and for its own part informative. It is an object of tacit** understanding; anyone seeing the image knows what its meaning is. It expresses something real yet precedent to commonplace reality, something from the prehistoric past, a fragment of essential divinity. Inaudibly it says to us something which becomes reality; it is communication antecedent to intellect and logic, it seizes on the peculiar and extraordinary. Where that occurs, the phenomenon has become myth. It has gained independent existence and in this sense it is irrelevant whether or not its representation is "art." The unicorn as an ideograph for Christ, and through Him as a symbol of the utmost purity which may at any time be attainable to man, has this power to survive all the vicissitudes of ebbing and flowing intensity.

Even today we feel the twentieth century is quite truly a century of the unicorn.

Just as was the case with the genesis of the Pieta, the written word precedes the sculptured or painted image (and of course the spoken word was precursor to the written one). First comes the word, and then the imagery follows in its train. Before the unicorn appeared in stone or other carvings it had been embodied in manuscripts. In the psalter it stands silently conspicuous in front of the psalmist; accompanied by the lion it menaces the crucified. This is something straight out of the Septuagint. Beside this is the effect of the original *Physiologus* which appeared chiefly in the eastern realm. In the psalter used in Hagia Sophia (the Christian Church of the Divine Wisdom, originally the Great Mosque, and now a museum) in Byzantium, the beast is seen confidently approaching the seated woman and placing its massive foot in her lap. In *Physiologus* the capture is in the first place pacific. Only later on does it develop, first in miniatures and then on capitals and choirstall carvings, into the cruel slaughter of the deluded beast.

In the plastic arts, the unicorn is at first the savage, alien, remote beast; but almost simultaneously the spiritual symbol made its appearance. However, in individual portrayal it is not always possible to make a proper differentiation. If the unicorn on the Souvigny pillar is to some extent unequivocally the monster from the Beyond, if the share of pagan and Christian strains in the Freudenstadt baptismal font is disputable (although some ritualistic background is discernible), yet in the Holzkirchen relief, the Christian tendency is indeed evident through the connection with the image of the Lord. The compelling impression left is that it had in every case a significant intensity for the spectators and might well have exerted a naturalistic or spiritual reality according to the individual case. [Ills. 14, 16, 23, 24, 53-55]

The harsh representation of the killing in the virgin's lap probably emanated from France, progressed into Italy and – more forcibly – into Germany. Apart from the bestiaries pure and simple, it was to be understood in the religious sense and its brutality was intentional; it was a depictment of the deicide. The unicorn gained its most powerful symbolic hold on **humanity in German mysticism, in the virgin-and-unicorn imagery, and in** the sacred hunt. Here in religious mystique, where otherwise a drift into perversion has not always been avoided, the unicorn maintained its spiritual character. This is so strong that it survived secularization and rationalization. [Ills. 45, 47, 72, 73]

The thrust toward demything in the ages of Reformation, Renaissance, and Enlightenment might quite possibly have destroyed the unicorn myth. **But it survived and not only in medical usage. The unicorn remained quite a long time also in the Church—in ancient images, despite the decrees of** the Council of Trent, in songs and ballads, and occasionally even in Protestant hymnbooks. Even late in the eighteenth century, Pacher, Abbot Benedict III of Ettal, had his heraldic device placed in the church: in front of the shrine of the Madonna and Child a unicorn makes obeisance. Evidently the abbot in contrition recognized himself as a rampageous unicorn like old Ratgar of Fulda, so dubbed centuries before by his friars.

Uneasy, often, was the user of unicorn references. When in Shakespeare's *Tempest* the passengers of the vessel stranded by Ariel stagger through the marvels and terrors of Prospero's island, one of them finally exclaims, "Now I will believe that there are unicorns." This does not sound exactly as though that enlightened author did believe in them. As we mentioned previosuly, Shakespeare most likely saw a representation of the unicorn in his local church in Stratford-on-Avon where later he was himself laid to rest, and he made poetic use of it on various occasions. In *Julius Caesar,* for example, Decius Brutus says (Act II, Sc. 1, 204) that "unicorns may be betray'd with trees," just as we have seen the lion and the brave little tailor do.

While the intellectual struggles were proceeding regarding the existence of the unicorn and its pharmaceutical value, the unicorn was transplanted to the southerly heaven. First is the appearance of the constellation in 1624 in the writings of Kepler's son-in-law Jacob Bartsch. Since he remarks, referring incidentally to various mentions of the unicorn in the Bible, that the constellation may have been so named "more recently" (*a recentioribus*), it seems that he himself did not propose that appellation. Ever since, however, we find the unicorn on the celestial globe.

Likewise in the seventeenth century the unicorn myth experienced a novel literary development. In the period from 1609 to 1627 Honoré d'Urfé's five-volume novel *L'Astrée* (Astraea), prototype of a long series of pastoral romances was published. The *Fontaine enchantée de la vérité d'amour* (Fountain Spring of True Love), guarded by lions and unicorns, plays a part in the tales. As the two couples, the chief characters in the story, despair of each other, the partners visit the magic spring separately for the purpose of casting themselves to the lions. Once there, however, they simultaneously recognize their true love and fidelity. They are attacked by the beasts – but the unicorns come to their assistance. The turmoil is hidden by a cloud and when this lifts again, the four lovers lie lifeless, yet unwounded, the animals are petrified statues around the spring, and Cupid appears over the scene announcing his orders to the spectators who have gathered round. The unicorn it seems has preserved itself as symbol for both love and death at the same time. But after Cupid's instructions are followed, those who had only swooned recover consciousness and the complications proceed until all finally ends happily. In the eighteenth century this dramatic scene of battle between lions and unicorns served N. C. Cochin for a decorative sketch, as indeed the widely distributed and long reverberative novel had **provided work for illustrators, not least with unicorns. [Ill. 161]**

Romanticism rescued not only images which had been thrown out of the churches but gave new life to the unicorn myth. It cannot be sheer chance that one of the loveliest unicorn poems in the German language comes to us from one of the publishers of *des Knaben Wunderhorn* (The Magic Horn). **This jewel of a poem lies unacknowledged in Achim von Arnim's novel** *Die Kronenwächter* **(The Guardians of the Crown), in which a young farmer thus** sublimates his nocturnal adventure with a dairymaid:

With sunbeams shining my pursuers,
Like unicorn free do I bound,
'Til even, away from my tortures,
To virgin's lap escape I've found,
To catch me with gossamer she knew,
But with the dawn she set me free,
On her lashes gazed I true,
But those sweet eyes she shut on me.

Eyes to the night
She opes anew.
O lustrous sight
Down falls the dew.
Shorter the days,
Longer the night,
Abates the woe
That wakes me quite.

Here again we have the familiar elements: the hunting of the unicorn, its flight to the damsel's lap, and from that Christian vestige, reversion to the spell of love, to which the Hindu ascetic had succumbed in his time, and **by which the bards, troubadours, and minnesingers themselves felt**

153. Sea unicorn and narwhal from Pomet's text on pharmacy

UNICORNS HORN

Now brought in Ufe for the Cure of Difeafes by an Experi
enced DOCTOR, the AUTHOR of this Antidote.

A Moſt Excellent Drink made with a true *Unicorns Horn*, which dotl
Effectually Cure theſe Diſeaſes :

Further, If any pleaſe to be
ſatisfied, they may come to the
Doctor and view the *Horn*.

Viz.

Scurvy, Old Ulcers,
Dropſie,
Running Gout,
Conſumptions, Diſtillations, Coughs
Palpitation of the Heart,
Fainting Fits, Convulſions,
Kings Evil, Rickets in Children,
Melancholly or Sadneſs,
The Green Sickneſs, Obſtructions,

And all Diſtempers proceeding from a Cold Cauſe.

The Uſe of it is ſo profitable, that it prevents Diſeaſes and Infection
by fortifying the Noble Parts, and powerfully expels what is an Enemy to
Nature, preſerving the Vigour, Youth, and a good Complexion to Old
Age : The Virtue is of ſuch force, as to reſiſt an Injury from an unſound
Bedfellow ; None can excel this, for it is joyned with the Virtue of a true
Unicorns Horn, through which the Drink paſſeth, and being impregnated
therewith, it doth wonderfully Corroborate and Cure, drinking it warm
at any time of the Day, about a quarter of a Pint at a time, the oftner the
better, the Price is 2 s. the Quart.

2. Alſo as a preparative for this excellent Drink, and good againſt the
Diſeaſes above mentioned, and all Crudities in the Body, is ready prepared twelve Pils in a Box to be taken at three Doſes, according to Directi-
ons therewith given, the Price is 2 s. the Box.

3. Likewiſe he hath Admirable Medicines for the Cure of the POX,
or Running of the Reins, with all Simptoms and Accidents thereto belonging, whether Newly taken or of long Continuance, and (by God's Bleſ-
ſing) ſecures the Patient from the danger of the Diſeaſe preſently, and
perfects the Cure with the greateſt Speed and Secreſie imaginable, not
hindering Occaſions, or going abroad : Whoſoever makes Uſe of theſe
Admirable Medicines, may have further Advice from the Doctor without
Charge.

The Doctor Liveth in Hounſditch, *next Door to* Gun-Yard, *have-*
ing a Back Door into the Yard, where any Patient may come pri

identified with the unicorn. The connection is so unmistakable that an old typographical error cannot change it. From the first edition of the *Guardians of the Crown* to its latest reprint, the second line of the poem in German contained the word Eichhorn ("squirrel"), instead of Einhorn ("unicorn"), indubitably the correct term. As the manuscript has disappeared, it cannot be established where the error arose, since Bettina published the second part of the novel from her husband's estate in 1854. But now the authentic version has been restored.

This poem remained long unique. In E. T. A. Hoffman's *Princess Brambilla*, a Roman capriccio based on sketches by the famous etcher Jacques Callot, a carnival procession is described moving through the Porta del Popolo to the Piazza Navona. Musicians with silver pipes, cymbals, and drums ride twelve small snow-white unicorns with golden hoofs drawing the lady's coach. It does not sound quite so playful when the duke of Coburg writes to the poet Jean Paul, "Tell yourself that I in the guise of a damsel can disarm the unicorn and that with a kiss." The unicorn fades away occasionally into a decorative figure of symbolic poesy and painting (as on a picture by the French painter Moreau). The Swiss Böcklin once more gives it a touch of vigor and mystery (his "Forest Silence" filled contemporaries at the end of the nineteenth century with enthusiasm). It satisfied part of the need of the Art Nouveau for ornamentation (imitating the Baroque, it guards the entrance to the Mirabell Park in Salzburg). The line leads on into the present time (the monster stands inoffensively as a plaything in front of boys' schools).

A picture painted by the American Arthur B. Davies in 1906 and now in the Metropolitan Museum, New York, shows a conceptualization related to the European symbolism. *Unicorns* is regarded as this painter's most famous picture and manifestly enjoys great popularity in the United States. Its sublime seascape and mountain scenery, girls and unicorns, all boldly lined and tranquil, create as a whole a mood of exaltation and repose.

The unicorn has again been given full power by Rainer Maria Rilke in that poem from his *Sonnets to Orpheus* that arose from the impression made on him by the Parisian tapestries of the "Lady with the Unicorn." Here "the beast that no existence hath," is acknowledged in its meaning and value, a creation of mankind, of the human soul, necessary for filling a particular void, indiscernible, all the more nonexistent for the secular, and becoming visible only in the silver speculum of the maidenly soul:

O here's the beast that no existence hath.
By sight they knew it not yet held it dear —
Its roaming, bearing and its bray not wrath,

154. Unnamed London doctor's poster from the seventeenth century

Even indeed the light of its soft leer.
Truly it never was. Yet through their love became
A taintless beast. For it, space ever freed.
And in that space, unhampered without claim,
Its head it nimbly raised with scarce a need
To be. They nourished it but not with corn,
But ever with the prospect, it might be,
And that gave so much vigor to the beast,
That from its brow there sprouted out a horn.
One unique horn. To virgin blamelessly
It came – In silvern mirror and in her to feast.

155. Sea unicorn, sixteenth century

The German philosopher Otto Friedrich Bollnow correlated the "beast that no existence hath" to Rilke's "Angel nonexistent" (in an outline for the *Duino Elegies*). According to this, "not only in the negative sense does that association imply something regarding the nonexistence of the angel, **but also from the diaphanous, ideal presentment of the unicorn it facilitates** understanding of the nature of the angel." This angel of Rilke's (not a Christian angel) "is a creature such as to assure recognition of a higher degree of reality in the invisible world," it is "that creation wherein the metamorphosis we are producing of the visible into the invisible seems to be already accomplished." Thus Bollnow interprets Rilke's phrase "Let the world be glorified for the angel!" as the demand "Glorify the world in comsummate spiritualization!" That is at the same time the finest possible thing to be said about the unicorn as a spiritual reality, which with repeated significance illuminates the history of the creature. *That* is how we may understand it and in this way it holds its ground in this strange, appalling era in which we are living, grappling so passionately for spiritualization of matter. This is a new Age of Reason and Intellect – but not that alone. It is appropriate that the unicorn is now as alive, as a spiritual symbol and poetic reality, as almost never before.

The unicorn makes mockery of time. The German poet Wilhelm Lehmann, who encountered Leda's swan and Europa's bull in the lakes and leas of Holstein, has also seen the lady on the unicorn. She descends from the Gobelin tapestry in the museum, is transformed into the woman driving her automobile over the asphalt of the avenue, and yet is still the same person who rides the legendary beast through the forest – a symbol of the interlacing of periods and realities which is often distinctive of Lehmann's poetic works. Oscar Loerke, who ranks so close to him, sketches the achromatic picture of the "Silver Forest" in which "no unicorn sets further foot," not even one unicorn! It is the kingdom of Death. The amateur of contemporary lyrics will have several further encounters with the animal, in various shapes and meanings, through works of such poets as Hilde Domin, Gertrud **Kolmar, Celan, Garcia Lorca, Klessmann, and others too numerous to list.** One or other old symbolic interpretations may also thus come to mind when, for example, Wolfdietrich Schnurre inquires: "Canst thou, O Death, not come as unicorn?" Why not pause to savor something of the poetic variety for ourselves?

'The Unicorn'
Lo! in the mute, mid wilderness,
What wondrous Creature? – of no kind! –
His burning lair doth largely press –
Gaze fixt – and feeding on the wind?
His fell is of the desert dye,
And tissue adust, dun-yellow and dry,
Compact of living sands; his eye
Black luminary, soft and mild,
With its dark lustre cools the wild;
From his stately forehead springs
Piercing to heaven, a radiant horn, --
Lo! the compeer of lion-kings!
The steed self-armed, the Unicorn!
Ever heard of, never seen,
With a main of sands between
Him and approach; his lonely pride
To course his arid arena wide,
Free as the hurricane, or lie here
Lord of his couch as his career! –
Wherefore should this foot profane
His sanctuary, still domain?
Let me turn, ere eye so bland
Perchance be fire-shot, like heaven's brand,
To whither my boldness! Northward now,
Behind the white star on his brow
Glittering straight against the sun,
Far athwart his lair I run.
           by George Darley

156. Fourteenth-century watermark

Based on the poem *Das Einhorn*
by Gertrud Kolmar

The Unicorn

The peacock's spread,
Blue, green and gold, flaunted in the twilight
Of tropic clamor in the treetops, and gray apes
Snapped their teeth and wrangled, swung and scuffled and
    wrestled in the foliage.
The mighty tiger lurking low with claws atwitch stared hard and
    tense,
As though his Indian forests streaked that silent unfamiliar game,
Westward to the sea.

The Unicorn

His hooves dashed on the rising tide,
Lightly with greatest ease. The waves pranced
Arrogantly,
And the pursuant, whinnying, silver-maned throng scoured
    onward and on and on.
Up above them.
A flight of black storks painted hasty signs of puzzlement on the
    Arabian heavens,
Which with the setting sun resembled a fruit-laden bowl:
Ripened pear and luscious rosy apple,
Peaches, oranges and magnificent grapes,
With wedges of ripe melon,
Black rocks lay a-glimmering in the gloaming,
Castles amethystine,
And enchanted palaces of carnelian and topaz glowed white,
Roseate mists hung late over the dovegrayed dark'ning waters of
    the bay.

Sand swirled in eddies from his hooves,
A silent dust cloud. He saw
Lonely cities faintly etched with domes and minarets, and the
    obelisks in the graveyards
Ranged mute beneath the repercussive moon.
He saw
Ruins, abandoned abodes, housing naught but phantoms in
    glist'ning obscurity
Beneath cold constellations.

157. Publisher's house seal by Melchior Lechter

Once the desert screech owl lured him on,
And far away jackals howled complainingly;
While hyenas laughed.
And at the entrance to the tent beneath the date palm
Dreamily the white Syrian dromedary raised his scrubby head, and
      so did ring his bell.
Past and done with is the unicorn.
For from distance far, from Ophir land of golden treasure, came its
      nimble, fleeting feet.
And from its eyes there glittered glances as of those serpents
      commanded by the magician's flute to undulate and dance
      and juggle,
Yet from the center of his brow that spiked horn lucent poured a
      gentler shining light,
Onto the bare hands and delicately shrouded breasts of the lady
Resting there
Between the manna shrubs.
Modest
Their hail
And the quiet luster of deep expectant eyes
And a sigh, a gentle swelling murmur from the muzzle,
Nighttime purling.

Unicorn
Such pleasure's
In this most discreet of beasts.
This unicorn mild

Treads so soft
One hears it not
Coming in, nor going;
Tame pet
of joy

When it's thirsty
It licks the teardrops
Out of fancies.
      Based on the poem *Einhorn*
      by Hilda Domin

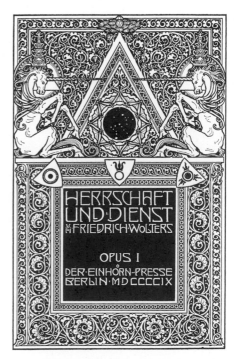

158. Melchior Lechter's title page for
Herrschaft und Dienst (Authority and
Service) by Friedrich Wolters

The Carline Thistle Coppice
Within the grove of thistle
My home lies deeply hid.
Pan stalked right by a-bristle.
Unto the end to wrestle
In night-dark form he did.

Pale thistles stand there rigid
In mourning, wild array.
A creak from roots there buried;
When we Pan's sleep have harried.
In his defense none play.

A blossom may have fallen there
For deeper communion
With him, to wither bare;
O father, thou'rt now my care,
I'm guarding thee, my son.

In woodland deep its hiding,
By softest light befired.
My heart – naught came a-riding,
No unicorn came striding –
My heart just beat inspired.

Based on the poem *Der Silberdistelwald*
by Oscar Loerke

Unicorn Hunt
On Merlin's mossgrown country lanes,
Through copse and rose-decked trellises,
Quietly trots a horde of spears,
Argent pennants, golden standards,
Saddlecloths of brazen color,
Flakes of plumes the branches powder.
A whippet pack scents out the trail,
A teasing tongue licks at the hooves
Of gentle palfreys delicate.
Tinkling laughter stirs ev'ry leaf
After the echo of men's strides,
The harnesses jingle gently.
And bannermen and armigers,
Pages, falconers and bowmen
Scout around to find their quarry:
Deeper still the standards flicker
A-sparkle in the coppices,
But silence darkens 'twixt the boles.
Fanned by the blowing of the horns
Every rose doth look on fire,
And crimson patches fool the pack.
Quietly has the game escaped
And its slender horn blows worldly
Thro' the verses which were woven:
Meshed network of the magic sports,
Wherein the hunters were involved,
Before they strayed in the forest.

Based on the poem *Unicorn Hunt*
by Eckart Klessmann

159. Sketch by Jean Cocteau
for "Lady with the
Unicorn" ballet

160.   Upper Austrian tarot card, nineteenth
century

LA FONTAINE ENCHANTÉE DE LA VERITÉ D'AMOUR.

Dédiée à Monsieur Alexandre Roslin, Chevalier de L'Ordre Royal de Vasa, Peintre ordinaire du Roi, Conseiller de son Académie de Peinture et Sculpture, de l'Académie Rle. de Stockholm &c.

161. Augustin de Saint-Aubin (after
Nicolas Cochin). Scene from Honoré
d'Urfé's pastoral romance *L'Astrée*
(Astaea)

Numerous American, English, French, and German novels use the unicorn in title or text – sometimes, of course, rather as a garnish or superficial token of something extraordinary, and occasionally from some real knowledge of its true significance. In Thomas Mann's novel *Der Erwählte* (The Elected Man), which describes a consanguineous love on medieval lines betwixt tragedy and satire, one of the courtiers bluntly insinuates, "Duke Wiligis may assuredly acquire some fame catching the unicorn when it dozes off in his innocent sister's bosom." Oscar Matzerath, the leading character in Günter Grass' *Die Blechtrommel* (The Tin Drum), discovers in a Danzig church a gayly colored figured tapestry suitable for a mural decoration. "The copy on rather antique pattern depicted a primly behaving lady with a fabulous animal, called a unicorn, subservient to her." It may be assumed that Matzerath's creator has seen the "rather antique pattern" in the Cluny Museum in Paris. (Matzerath draws comparisons between the submissiveness of the unicorn to the woman woven in the tapestry, and that of his gangster underlings to Lucie the gang queen – but reserves to himself alone the right to be "the solitary creature with the excessively spiroid horn.") While here it is only a side issue, the erotic element of the unicorn story steps commandingly and meaningfully to the fore in Martin Walser's novel titled with the name of the legendary creature, yet on a background of accurate knowledge of the other unicorn connotations. Walser has mentioned that he first came across the unicorn in the works of Suso. "Whoever has caught the savage unicorn if not thyself" is the way that medieval mystic addresses the Virgin Mary.

Ernst Fuchs, painter and illustrator of the Viennese school of "imaginative realism," repeatedly grapples with the configuration and meaning of the unicorn. When he says, "its horn is purest light, as though of cut glass," he absolutely does not have to be aware that Rudolf von Ems said of this horn that it is "just like a glass." But he obviously knows the numerous links to the fabulous creature and formulates a modern version when he says, "The horn between its eyes is also its all-penetrating spirit." The twentieth century has accepted the unicorn tradition and added thereto the conversion into pure spirit.

It is in this double sense of tradition and a new understanding that America has taken over the unicorn, one of the most amazing events in the migratory story of this versatile creature. Highly characteristic in this context is the application of the unicorn in Tennessee Williams' play *The Glass Menagerie*. The play's heroine Laura, physically disabled by the vestiges of polio and psychially impaired to the verge of pathological breakdown by her unrequited, unperceived love for Jim, unable to cope with reality, has bestowed her whole affection on an object congenial to her vulnerable sensitivity: a collection of small glass animals. Among these is a unicorn, her favorite—she identifies with the animal, as aloof and peculiar as she appears in her own eyes. During one of his visits to her, Jim clumsily lets the unicorn fall on the floor, and it loses its horn as a result. It is now as impaired as Laura, who herself is torn out of her dream world by this new encounter with her secret beloved and has lost her imagined uniqueness. She gives the unicorn, now just an ordinary animal like any other, to Jim as a final parting gift "for remembrance."

Whether Laura is herself liberated from her trauma by this act of surrogation is left for our further reflection. Yet we cannot help but recollect that the unicorn as a figure for Christ also comes remarkably close to the ancient Jewish scapegoat which was driven forth laden with the sins of mankind. Certainly here the ancient myth has gained another facet, just by being refracted through the intellect and passing through the detective process of modern psychological research. This takes place in a poetic manner apparently not grasped by or at least not utilized by the Viennese school of psychology. C. G. Jung in his *Psychology and Alchemy* textbook devoted a special chapter to the unicorn, but it handled the subject historically without adding anything really new.

That the transposition into creative allegory should have happened just in America is a matter worthy of reflection. This is but one example – an important one, but not the only significant one – of the fact that the unicorn in its agelong peregrination followed universal stress and strain from the orient through to Europe and now even to the New World. It seems appropriate that the unicorn's loveliest portrayal, that last tapestry of the set in The Cloisters, should have come to America. Poetic reality of the unicorn in America embraces the whole of its past. In his *New Year Letter,* W. H. Auden addresses the Lord in various forms, including that of a unicorn:

> O unicorn among the cedars
> To whom no magic charm can lead us,
> White childhood moving like a sigh
> Through the green woods unharmed in thy
> Sophisticated innocence
> To call thy true love to the dance . . .

What abundance of reference in a few lines. The unicorn is hidden among cedars in an oriental forest. Magic does not lead to it, only belief and meditation, for it is a pure spirit hovering lightly as breath. It is a child, *the* child, in whom the antitheses of Thought and Belief converge. It possesses childlike innocence, but a sophisticated innocence, pensive and intellectual. This unicorn representing piety has passed through rationalism, like the devout writer himself who united the contrasts in his own person and represented a bridge between the old world and the new as understood spatially and temporally.

The unicorn lends itself even to pressing sociopolitical questions in the United States. A black writer, Dudley Randall, in discussion with a white critic who advises him not to write on controversial issues, on liberty and homicide, but on timeless questions and symbols such as the white unicorn, retorts with the query, "A white unicorn? Does it believe in integration? And why not a black unicorn?" There's nothing apolitical, nothing timeless, unless it's dead. But the unicorn is alive.

Twice the unicorn provided material for a ballet. Jean Cocteau, who has sketched it many a time in fanciful form, even as a cuckolded human, took as his theme the Paris tapestries, with musical score by Jacques Chailley. "The theme," he himself wrote, "is virginal purity. According to the legend, the unicorn takes food only from the hand of a virgin. The mirror in which the damsel shows him his face, also shows the reflection of another visage, that of the knight who brings her human love. The unicorn sees it and dies."

The Italian-American composer Gian Carlo Menotti lyricizes the unicorn. With two other legendary Gothic monsters, gorgon and manticore, it embodies the fanciful ideas with which the writer lives misunderstood in the workaday world, which he apparently betrays and which yet are the only ones to attend his deathbed. They all live endangered in this world. The writer must warn his unicorn against the virgin, who feigns to be sleeping beneath the tree but is the decoy with which the hunter intends to catch the unicorn. Thus here again the circle of references comes to a close, with ancient myth and modern intellectualism merging together.

The ancient monster which passed through so many forms is about to experience a new renaissance. It seems immortal because it is versatile. Something which Schiller did not directly coin on his crest may nevertheless validly apply to it:

> *What in past days nowhere came to pass*
> *That alone doth never age.*

Unicorn Bibliography

The best starting point for a methodical pursuit of the unicorn is the definitive contribution on the legendary animal by Liselotte Wehrhahn-Stauch in the *Reallexikon zur Deutschen Kunstgeschichte* (Encyclopedia of the History of German Art), 4, Stuttgart, 1958. Despite its scope it needed some concentration to do full justice to the abundance of literary and econographic material (and anyone who thinks he has discovered something new will do well to recheck whether such discovery is not already included in this superlative essay). Of almost equal excellence is H. Brandenburg's article "Einhorn" ("Unicorn") in the *Reallexikon fur Antike und Christentum* (Encyclopedia of Antiquity and Christianity), 4, Stuttgart, 1959, the importance of which rests especially in its thorough exploration of the patristic fathers, though placing this aspect in a general context. Regarding antiquity, all questions on subject and personal keywords (unicorn, Physiologus, Ctesias, Megasthenes, Aelian, Pliny, etc.) should be referred to Pauly-Wissowa's *Real-Encyclopadie der klassischen Altertumswissenschaft* (Practical Encyclopedia of Classical Archaeology), Stuttgart, 1894-1903. And for supplementing these sources one may well turn to the manuals on German superstition, German legends, and particularly the guidebooks to ecclesiastical iconography.

All these sources give a wealth of literary reference which allows us to condense considerably the bibliographic details now following and to limit ourselves to especially significant publications and a few individual supplements. Some inspiration may be gained from consultation of general reference works such as the comprehensive eighteenth-century universal encyclopedia *Grosses Universallexikon* published by J. H. Zedler, Halle and Leipzig, or by pursuing from edition to edition the unicorn articles varying in succeeding issues of famous encyclopedias.

The fundamental texts of classical Greek and Latin antiquity are available in the Oxford series *Scriptorum classicorum bibliothecae oxoniensis*, Oxford, 1900 etc. Those of the Church Fathers and other Christian writers from the earliest days of Christianity down to the late Middle Ages are in the multivolume collections *Patrilogiae cursus completus, Patrologia graeca* (approximately 160 volumes, 1886 etc.) and *Patrologia latina* (approximately 200 volumes, 1844 etc.) published by Jacques Paul Migne and his successors, in Paris. *Physiologus* is available in an attractive and inexpensive German translation excellently written by Otto Seel for the *Lebendige Antike* (Living Antiquity) series. A broad selection on the basis of various ancient texts, a style which comprises the charm of the original, a superb introduction with critical commentaries and literary references can similarly delight the scientific researcher and the amateur concerned with studying the history of civilization. Both will enjoy the especially handsome facsimile edition of *Physiologus Bernensis,* Basel, 1964, a manuscript from the era of the Carolingian Renaissance, with accompanying translation of the text into German and scientific commentary thereon. Francisco Sbordone's *Physiologus*, Milan, 1936, "attains with regard to the Greek text the highest peak of what is possible and of what can be reasonably expected" (Seel); but Sbordone's work was published without any table of contents and the index is incomplete. The importance of Sbordone's work appears in a different language after the lapse of a few decades, when that deficiency was remedied in Henkel and Schoene, *Emblemata*, Stuttgart, 1967, which contains an improved index to Sbordone's edition of *Physiologus*.

Among monographic treatises on our subject, one of the older texts is quite valuable, namely Carl Cohn's *Zur literarischen Geschichte des Einhorns* (On a Literary History of the Unicorn) which appeared in two parts as supplements to the *Annual Transactions of the Berlin City Realschule*, 11 (Easter 1896 and 1897). Among more up-to-date treatises, a special place must be accorded to Odell Shepard's *The Lore of the Unicorn*, London, 1930, reprinted 1967 without amendment. The subject is elaborated with typical English combination of scholarship, fluency, and sense of the picturesque. A particular feature of the volume is the detailed discussion of the scientific controversy which raged at the beginning of the modern age regarding the unicorn and its medical virtues. But the book is not just valuable for that alone, even though it does not go beyond the state of affairs in 1930 and is somewhat deficient in iconography. One special area, though always with a glance at the unicorn problem as a whole is covered by Richard Ettinghausen's "The Unicorn," *Studies in Muslim Iconography*, 1, Washington, 1950, which is unique in depiction of the unicorn and its significance in the Arabian Middle Ages.

As to the ecclesiastical appropriation of the unicorn, special attention should be paid to the illustration of a particularly venerable ritual usage (on a ninth-century fan) in Lorenz E. A. Eitner's "The Flabellum of Tournus," *The Art Bulletin Supplement*, New York, 1944. A text which will be certainly for a long time to come definitive is the voluminous dissertation of the Franciscan Father, Dr. Jürgen W. Einhorn, titled *Spiritalis unicornis – The Unicorn as a Transmitter of Meaning in Medieval Literature and Art*, Munich: Fink, 1976. Apart from linguistic difficulty, its bulk (almost 600 pages) makes it difficult for the interested layman, yet it is indispensable for its solid scholarship. Numerous individual investigations and essays (as well as references to many pictorial illustrations of the unicorn) are obtainable from the foregoing literature; some are mentioned selectively in relation to the individual items. For the general correlation of animal illustration in the middle ages and in the first centuries of the modern era, with numerous special references also to the unicorn, *Studium generale* in its twentieth volume, Berlin, 1967, published two informative papers, namely in no. 4, "Animal Portrayal in the Middle Ages," by Paul Girkon, and in no. 5, "Animal Illustration in the Fifteenth and Sixteenth Centuries" by Herbert Schade.

A Fascinating Figment
Hocke, Gustav René. "Die Welt als Labyrinth." *Manierismus* (Hamburg) 1 (1957): 193.

Reports from the East
Berg, Bengt. *Meine Jagd nach dem Einhorn* (My Hunt for the Unicorn). Frankfurt am Main, 1931. See also *Sutta Nipata*, O.U.P., 1889, 7-15.
Keller, Otto. *Die antike Tierwelt* (The Ancient Animal Kingdom), vol. 1. Leipzig, 1909. 415 *et seq.;* Gryphius, Andreas. *Gedicthe* (Poetry), vol. 3. Darmstadt: 1961. 533.
Wilhelm, Richard. "The Unicorn in China." *Der Ostasiatische Lloyd*, vol. 25. Shanghai, 1911. 539 *et seq.*

The Biblical Beast
On Abbot Ratgar, see Simson, Bernhard, *Jahrbücher des Fränksichen Reiches unter Ludwig dem Frommen* (Annals of the Frankish Empire Under Louis the Pious). Leipzig, 1874. 371 *et seq.;* Brouwerus, Christopherus. *Fuldensium Antiquitatum*, vol. 3. Antwerp, 1612. 88 *et seq.*
Dähnhardt, Oskar, ed., *Natursagen*, vol. 1. Leipzig, 1907. 287.
Migne, J. P., ed. *Patrologia latina:* Honorius of Aachen. Paris. *ca.* 1844. 122.
On the consequences of the Byzantine unicorn legend in medieval Russian cloisters, see Rybakov, B. A. *Die angewandte Kunst der Kiewer Rus im 9. bis 11. Jh. und der südrussischen Fürstentümer im 12./13. Jh.* (Applied Art of the Kiev Ros in the ninth to eleventh centuries and of the Ukrainian Principalities in the twelfth to thirteenth centuries). Dresden, 1957.

Tales from Physiologus
The oldest German version of *Physiologus* appears in *Denkmäler deutscher Poesie und Prosa aus dem VIII-XII Jh.*(Landmarks in German Prose and Poetry from the Eighth to the Twelfth Centuries), ed. by Müllenhoff and Scherer, 3rd ed. by Steinmeyer, vol. 1, Berlin, 1892, 263. Further German sources of particular importance are: Albertus Magnus, *De animalibus libri XXVI*, in accordance with the original Cologne text, Münster: Hermann Stadler, vol. 1 (1916), vol. 2 (1921). Conrad von Megenberg's *Das Buch der Natur*, ed. Hugo Schulz, Greifwald, 1897, 133, and Rudolf van Ems' *Weltchronik*, ed. Gustav Ehrismann, Berlin, 1915. Outstanding

bestiaries are Guillaume le Clerc's *Le Bestiaire*, ed. Reinsch, Leipzig, 1892, with comprehensive introduction covering a critique of sources; Richard de Fournival's *Le Bestiaire d'amour*, ed. Hippeau, Paris 1860. See also the Hamburg Museum for Art and Industry Exhibition Catalog *Bestiarium* 162, and similar publications of British and American museums of history and the arts.

On the story of the hermit Unicorn and the aftermath of the legend according to the latest researches and current collation with more ancient sources, see Dieter Schlingloff's article "Die Einhornlegende" (The Unicorn Legend), *Christiana Albertina* (Kiel University Journal), November 1971.

On the fable of the man in the well, see Ernst Kuhn's article "Barlaam und Joasaph," in *Transactions of the Royal Bavarian Academy of Science Faculty of Philological Philosophy* (in German), vol. 20 (1897); Ewald Vetter's article "Media Vita," in *Collected Essays on the History of Spanish Civilization* (in German), Münster, 1960; the "Legenda Aurea" (Golden Legend) by Giacopo di Voragine is available in various editions, of which the version by Richard Benz, Jena, 1925, was used for this book. The Bundahish, ed. Ferdinand Justi, Leipzig, 1868.

Monstrous Symbols
Bernheimer, Richard. *Romanische Tierplastik.* Munich, 1931. von Blankenburg, Vera. *Heilige und damonische Tiere.* Leipzig, 1943, 146 *et seq.* on the Freudenstadt font.

Male, Emile. *L'Art religieux au XIIe siecle en France.* 5th ed. Paris, 1947, 323 *et seq.* on the Souvigny pillar; other volumes of Male's great iconographic work on twelfth-century French religious art are important sources on unicorn questions.

Schade, Herbert, *Dämonen und Monstren.* Regensburg, 1962, 69 *et seq.* regarding Freudenstadt.

"Legendary Animals" are comprehensively covered by Salome Zajadacz-Hastenrath in the German art history encyclopedia *Reallexikon zur deutschen Kunstgeschichte* vol. 6.

The Road to Mysticism (and) The Celestial Hunt
Francis of Retz. *Defensorium inviolatus virginitatis Mariae. Ca.* 1400. Facsimile reproduction, Weimar, 1910.
Alain of Lille (Alanus ab insulis). *Patrologia latina* (PL 210). Migne, In addition to Wehrhahn-Stauch's article in the *Reallexikon zur deutschen Kunstgeschichte*, previously mentioned, the extensive literature under this heading includes Brigitte Klesse's "Das Niederzündurfer Antependium mit der allegorischen Einhornjagd," which takes this noteworthy individual work as its starting point in *Unser Porz*, no. 6, 1964.
Unicorn poems: Uhland, Ludwig, ed. *Alte hoch- und niederdeutsche Volkslieder* (Old High and Low German Folksongs), vol. 2, nos. 320, 338, and 339; Böhme, Franz M. *Altdeutsches Liederbuch* (Old

German Songbook). 3rd ed. Leipzig, 1925. Nos. 598, 603; Erk, Ludwig. *Deutscher Liederhort* (A Garden of German Song). Leipzig, 1925. Vol. 3, no. 2145.

On the Marian symbols, see especially Salzer, Anselm, *Die Sinnbilder and Beiworte Mariens in der deutschen Literatur und Hymnenpoesie des Mittelalters* (Symbols and Epithets of the Virgin Mary in Medieval German Literature and Hymn Lyrics). Reprint Darmstadt, 1967. On the unicorn, pages 44 *et seq.* but also to be consulted on the symbolic language in the illustrations of the Mystic Unicorn Hunt.

Hellmuth Graff's theses on old German art illustration of the sacred unicorn hunt, *Die Darstellungen der sakralen Einhornjagd in der altdeutschen Kunst*, delivered in Münster in 1923 and though not then printed, were a basic and still are a quite important source, which is now available through film reproduction, at Münster University.

The peculiar Swiss tapestry with Adam as slayer of the unicorn has been sketched and described by Robert L. Wyss in the Swiss **journal for archaeology and art history,** *Schweizerische Archäologie und Kunstgeschichte*, vol. 20, pts. 2/3, 1960, in his article "Vier Hortus-Conclusus-Darstellungen im Schweizerischen Landesmuseum" (Four illustrations of the *Hortus conclusus* in the Swiss National Museum).

Karl von Spiess's *Marksteine der Volkskunst* **(Milestones of Popular Art), pt. 2, Berling, 1942, contains a compendious chapter** of helpful material including illustrations on the subject of the unicorn hunt. In his interpretation the author endeavors to establish linkages with old German traditions. He traces the evolution of the unicorn hunt – cognate to deer hunting – from the nordic cycle of myths and legends. Just as the pursued doe in the popular ballad turns into a maiden, so too, says Spiess, the representations of the unicorn hunt are really metamorphoses in pictures in which the Virgin Mary makes a two-fold appearance as animal and as a damsel. The whole story then might well have been given a new Christian interpretation by the Church. The *hortus conclusus* or fenced garden is to Spiess a "place sacred to old nordic tradition." This might however seem to be an extremely biased exaggeration of the mythological details present in the "Wild Chase."

Marian symbols in the Hortus conclusus

In the "mystic hunt," the unicorn becomes one more of the numerous symbols for the Virgin and her virtues, the majority of which symbols are derived not from the New but from the Old Testament. The following notes should be welcome to anybody desirous of understanding such metaphoric language.

The *hortus conclusus* (fenced garden), like the "fountain sealed" in the *Song of Solomon* 4:12, is itself a symbol for Mary's maidenhood; the verse in question reads thus: "A garden inclosed is my

sister, my spouse; a spring shut up, a fountain sealed." Even the plants in that garden represent individual qualities of the Virgin, as again in the work of Alain de Lille "the myrtle of moderation, the role of patience, the lily of chastity, the violet of eternal introspection" (Migne, PL 210). In addition to the rose and the lily, the olive branch also appears as a token of virginity, and again we may refer to the *Song of Solomon* 2:2, "As the lily among thorns, so is my love among the daughters." In Luther's version the lily (not too unnaturally) becomes a rose.

Other portions of the Old Testament which have been interpreted as predictions relating to the Virgin Mary and which appeal in the illustrations of the "mystic unicorn hunt" are:

Closed gate: *Ezekiel* 44:1, ". . . This gate shall be shut, it shall not be opened, and no man shall enter in by it; because the Lord, the God of Israel hath entered in by it."

Burning Bush: *Exodus 3*. **From the burning bush unconsumed by** the flame, God gave Moses the task of leading his people out of Egypt.

Gideon's Fleece: *Judges* 6:36 *et seq.* Gideon, ordered by God to deliver the people of Israel from the oppression of the Midianites asked for a sign to confirm his mission – a sheep-skin which he spread on the floor of his barn to be moistened by the dew overnight whilst all the ground around remained dry (and when that did happen, he took the precaution of asking for and receiving the reverse phenomenon – for the fleece to remain dry while the surrounding ground was bedewed).

Aaron's Rod: *Numbers* 17. Of twelve rods each from one of the twelve tribes, Aaron's alone blossomed thus indicating that he was the elected high priest.

The Golden Pot: *Exodus* 16. The pot in which the manna was gathered. (According to Paul's *Epistle to the Hebrews* 9:4, this was a "golden pot.")

The Ark of the Covenant: *Exodus* 31:7. It carried salvation within it.

The Ivory Tower (or Tower of David): *Song of Solomon* 4:4, "Thy neck is like the tower of David builded for an armory."

The Well of Living Waters: *Song of Solomon* 4:15.

The Sun and Moon: *Song of Solomon* 6:9, "Who is she that looketh **forth as the morning, fair as the moon, clear as the sun . . ."** Jacob's Star: *Numbers* 24:17, ". . . there shall come a Star out of **Jacob, and a Sceptor shall rise out of Israel."**

Compare also in this context the twelfth-century hymn to the Virgin Mary, *Marienlied*, from Melk Abbey (Austria) in *Deutsche Lyrik des Mittelalters, no.* 1 (Medieval German Lyrics and Ballads), selected and modernized by Max Wehrli. Zurich, 1955. 8 *et seq.* This hymn enumerates various Marian symbols but does not mention the unicorn.

On the Diffusion of the "Mystic Hunt"

Some additions to the details in the text to explain the expansion of the "mystic hunt" motif may be of specific interest to traveling art lovers, although these notes lay no claim to exhaustive perfection. In particular, we cannot give an accurate accounting of possible losses of such art treasures during the war.

In Thüringen, the region of origin, Erfurt has five pictures, Weimar three, and Tonndorf near Weimar a further one. Then there are others in Allendorf, Gosskochberg, and Kaulsburg. In what was once the kingdom and later the province of Saxony, Aschersleben has some fretwork screens and an altar (which was for some time in Berlin), and several woven tapestries which appear to have been a favorite motif for needlework in the erstwhile Dambeck convent, just as in the southern Saxon nunneries where the mystic hunt was a popular subject. Several such pieces were produced, for example, in Isenhagen. Examples of southern Saxon textiles of this kind are now in the Brunswick and Hanover museums. The vane of an altar from Oldendorf in Hesse and now housed in the Marburg University Museum is held to be of south Saxon origin. Some items found in Silesia may be assumed to derive from central German models: carved altars in Bralin and Breslau, a painting in Görlitz. Other items of similar inspiration are to be found in the Brandenburg Marches (at Wilsickow), in Mecklenburg .at Lübbersdorf and Parchim), and in Lübeck cathedral (currently in St. Anne's Museum). On Grimmenthal, refer to Evans, E. P. *Animal Symbolism in Ecclesiastic Architecture.* London 1896. 103 *et seq.* Also (with reference to Father Dr. Jürgen Werinhard Einhorn): von Hintzenstern, Herbert. *Der Kreuzaltar in Gräfentonna* (Altar of the Crucifixion in Gräfentonna). East Berlin, 1957. 88 *et seq.*

The second spacious area of expansion is formed by the Upper Rhineland plains and the Alps. From the items in Mülhausen and Colmar, the altar from the Schongauer school now in the Unterlinden Museum in Colmar attracts particular attention; it was painted for the Dominican cloister, now also including a museum. Brigitte Klesse speculates that the Schongauer picture may have served as the model for three antependia which may have issued at long intervals—between the end of the fifteenth to the beginning of the sixteenth century—apparently from one and the same central Rhineland atelier; this is a question of applique embroideries (now in the Art and Crafts Museum in Cologne, and also in the Diocesan museums in Cologne and Limburg). The antependium in the Church of St. Mary's at Gelnhausen is most likely also of Rhenish origin—a restored mural is in the parish church of St. George's in Traunstein.

A set of south German designs is now in the Bavarian National Museum, Munich. In Carinthia, there is a carved wooden altar in Klagenfurt Provincial Museum, an altar painting in Friesach in the Tyrol, an oil painting in the Wilten Abbey, murals in Auffenstein Castle near Matrei, an altar in Stams cloister, a very faded mural in the transept of Brixen Minster, wooden figures (Virgin and unicorn only, probably the remains of an altar showing the hunting scene) in Karneid fortress near Bolzano.

As stated in our earlier chapters, such abundance is mainly in Germany; in contrast there are only a few examples in foreign countries. The mystic hunt is shown in the setting of the Burning Bush by Nicolas Froment made for the Magdalene Church a Aix-en-Provence, 1475. Also in France, there is a stained glass representation of this subject at Bourges. The most striking foreign example in this connection is the mural in St. Peter the Martyr's in Verona, Italy, a worthy supplement to the German canon. The painted ceiling at Hattula in Finland has already been mentioned in the text of this chapter.

Eye Witnesses

Itinerarius Johannis de Hese presbiterii . . . first published in Cologne, 1490. Our description of the unicorn story is somewhat more detailed, probably because it is based on a later printing, according to Raumer's Historical Notebook, series 4, vol. 8 (1867), 225. Arturo Graf (*Miti* 'Myths', vul. 1, 1893, reprinted Bologne 1965) is of the opinion that John of Hesse never left Utrecht.

Von Breydenbach, Bernard. *Reise ins Heilige Land* (Journey to the Holy Land). Mainz, 1486. Ernst Otto, Count of Solms-Laubach, devoted an article in the Städel Annual for 1935–1966 (Frankfurt) to the evidence that Reuwich the woodcarver and the "master recorder" of the art history are one and the same person. The same journey described by Faber, Felix. *Evagatorium in Terrae Sacrae, Arabiae et Egypti Perigrationum.* Stuttgart: Hassler, 1843 1849. vol. 2, 441.

Ingo Saymisch of Quedlinburg was kind enough to give me the particulars regarding the "unicorn skeleton" reconstructed by Otto von Guericke. Professor Karl Rode of Aachen gave me the reference to the elasmotherium. See: Neumayr, M. *Erdgeschichte* (Geology), vol. 2. Leipzig and Vienna, 1855. 448 *et seq.*

The Costly Horn

Miller, Genevieve. "The Unicorn in Medical History." In *Transactions and Studies of the College of Physicians of Philadelphia.* vol. 28 (1960), 80-93; contains bibliographic references, particularly but not exclusively, to the medical significance of the unicorn.

Boullet, Jean. "La merveilleuse histoire de la Licorne" (The Remarkable History of the Unicorn). In *Aesculape.* vol. 42 (December 1959); contains numerous illustrations and not always quite accurate quotations.

Marini, Andreas. *Discorso contra la falsa Opinione dell' Alicorno* (Address on the False Assessment of the Unicorn). Venice, 1566. Bacci, Andrea. *Discorso dell' Alicorno* (Discourse on the Unicorn). Florence, 1566. The copy used for the present work was a 1582 impression, also printed in Florence.

Parz, Affibroise. *Textes Choisis*. ed. Luis Delaruelle and Marcel Sendrail. Paris, 1953. This collection of selected writings by Parz (1517-1590) contains a number of his writings on the unicorn.

Bartholin, Thomas. *De unicornu observationes novae* (New Notes on the Unicorn). Padua, 1645.

Pomet, Pierre. *Histoire générale des drogues* (General History of Drugs). Paris, 1694. For this book we referred to the German *Aufrichtiger Materialist und Spezereihändler* (Honest Druggists and Grocers), Leipzig, 1717.

Compare statements by Liselotte Wehrhahn-Stauch in the RDK and Shepard's *The Lore of the Unicorn* for reconstruction of the unicorn controversy, pp 155 *et seq.* and also its preceding chapter (occasionally inexact as to details).

On the merit of the horn and the conflict as to its coming from the narwhal, see also Guido Schönberger in the Städel Annual (Frankfurt) for 1935-1936 (Course of prices, p. 214).

On the narwhal's tusk see Bernhard Peyer's *Die Zähne* (Teeth), Berlin, 1963, 76.

Hovorka, O. and Kronfeld, A. *Vergleichende Volksmedizin* (comparative Folk Remedies), vol. 1. Stuttgart, 1908. 114 *et seq.*, 323 *et seq.*

Hildegard of Bingen, after Migne's *Patrologia latina*, vol. 197.

Gesner, Conrad. *Historia Animalium* (vol. 4, Frankfurt (in German): *Tierbuch* (Bestiary)), Zurich, 1563, 35 *et seq.*

Grosses Universallexikon, vol. 8. Halle and Leipzig: Johann Heinrich Zedler, 1714; see under "Einhorn" (Unicorn) and also vol. 7, "Dens elephantis petrefactus" (Petrified elephant's tusk).

C. G. Jung in his *Psychology and Alchemy*, 2nd ed., Zurich, 1952, devoted an entire chapter to the unicorn with numerous quotes and illustrations. On page 591 of the German edition he interprets the unicorn, as well as the lion, as "the savage, unrestrained masculine, penetrating power of the *spiritus mercurialis*," confirming thus also in his view the erotic side of the unicorn myth. The "Chymical Wedding" of Christian Rosencreutz, Strassburg, 1616, the unicorn symbol wherein is Jung's starting point (cf. also Adolf Ammerschlager, "The Unicorn" in *Goetheanum*, vol. 7 (1928), 253 *et seq.;* it is not used as a source for our text, since the importance of same is, to say the least, apparently controversial.

On the pharmaceutical use of the unicorn in modern times: Wagner, M. I. "Phallus, Horn and Fish." In *Romanica Helvetica*, vol. 4 (Jubilee edition for Karl Jaberg), 1937.

I must express my thanks also to Elisabeth Korn, authoress of a historical presentation of the Duisburg Unicorn Pharmacy (Annals of the Lower Rhineland Historical Society, nos. 151/152) (1952) for valuable references regarding other relevant items in addition to the apothecary dispensaries. S. Gutmann has written a helpful compendium of the more than 100 unicorn pharmacies in the two German States, published by Spitzner, Ettlingen near Karlsruhe Baden.

On Helm and Scutcheon

The story of Sir Lelaing is related in the *Livre des faits de messire Jacques de Lelaing,* by some author whose identity is not definitely known, in Georges Chastellain's *Oeuvres*, vol. 8. Brussels: Kervyn de Lettenhove, 1868.

Von Eschenbach, Wolfram. *Parzival*, verses 613, 622. On Schiller's crest, see: Kühn, Adelbert. *Schiller*, vol. 1. Weimar, 1859, 120 *et seq.* On the British coat of arms, see: London, H. Standford. *Royal Beasts*. East Knoyle, Wiltshire, 1952.

Mulder, T. R. "Hoorns Hoorn en de Enhorn" (Hoorn's Horn and the Unicorn). In *West Frieslands Oud en Nieuw* (the Dutch Historical Society's publication, "Old West Friesland"), pt. 24, place and year of publication not given, 34-35. Contains various illustrations and references, principally but not exclusively to Dutch bibliography of the subject. The quotation from Charles V is mentioned in Guido Schönberger's abundantly documented article on his more selected subject *Narwhal-Unicorn, Studies on a rare material*. In the Städel Annual for 1935/1936, 167-247.

Wild Men and Women's Wiles

Quotation from the Arabic writer al-Tawhidi (who died some time later than A.D. 1010) in Ettinghausen, *op. cit.*, 60. On the erotic elements of the unicorn fable in French bestiaries, see Reinsch, Guillaume le Clerc, and Hippeau, Richard de Fournival. *Leonardo da Vinci: Diaries and Sketches*. Leipzig, 1952. 837 *et seq.* "Zoology" including a unicorn as symbol of intemperance.

On the Wild Men, see especially Richard Bernheimer's *Wild Men in the Middle Ages*. Cambridge, Massachusetts: Harvard University Press, 1952. *Wild Men in the Middle Ages,* exhibition catalog of the Museum for Art and Industry, Hamburg, 1963. On the Upper Rhineland wild men tapestries, see Hans Lanz's *Gotische Bildteppiche* (Gothic Figured Tapestries), Bern, 1955. On Dürer's *Abduction on the Unicorn*, see Bernheimer, 134 *et seq.;* Panofsky, Erwin, *Studies in Iconology*. New York, 1967, 85. Also Panofsky's *Albrecht Durer*, vol. 1. London, 1948, 196, and in the same volume 189 *et seq.* on Emperor Maximilian's Prayer Book.

My Sole Desire

The famous Parisian tapestries were discussed by the custodians of Cluny Museum, Pierre Verlet and Francis Salet, in the handsome illustrated volume *The Lady with the Unicorn*, Paris, 1960. Maria Lanckorovska upholds her thesis that Margaret of York was "the Lady with the Unicorn" in *Wandteppiche for eine Forstin* (Mural Tapestries for a Princess), Frankfurt, 1965. Sharply at variance in every respect with the authoress' learned disquisition, Francis Salet in *Bulletin Monumental*, vol. 122, 418 *et seq.*, cf. also vol. 123, 160 *et seq.* Considering the subject from the angle of the history of costumes, Barbara Purrucker also rejects the Lanckorovska theory in a lecture "On the Dating of the 'Lady with the Unicorn' Gobelins" to the Berlin Heraldry Society "Herold" on November 7, 1976 (unpublished). Numerous bibliographic references in Lanckorovska. See also Sophie Schneebalg-Perelmann "La Dame à la Licorne a été tissze a Bruxelles" (The Lady with the Unicorn was woven at Brussels) in *Gazette des Beaux Arts*, November 1967, 153-178.

Also relevant to this section is *Le romans de la Dame a la Lycorne et du beau Chevalier au Lyon* (The Tale of the Unicorn Lady and the Noble Lion Knight), published by Gennrich, Dresden, 1909. The marriage of Charles the Bold with Margaret of York is described in Olivier de La Marche's *Memoires*, vol. 2. Paris, 1883-1888. 101-201. Cf. also Otto Cartellieri. *At the Court of the Duke of Burgunny* (in German). Basel, 1926. 167 *et seq.*

Captured Yet Free

The magnificent collection of tapestries *The Hunting of the Unicorn*, an outstanding feature of The Cloisters, New York, has been still further enhanced by the explanations and interpretations published by the New York Metropolitan Museum of Art, especially in the following texts:
Rorimer, James J. *The Unicorn Tapestries at the Cloisters*. 1962. *The Picture Book of the Unicorn Tapestries*. 1944/5. *On the Flowers of the Unicorn Tapestry*, published by the Bronx Botanical Gardens.
Brandford and Weigert. *The French Tapestries*. England, 1962. Worthy also of attention are the commentaires in the now out-of-print Catalog of the Tapestry Exhibition, *Masterpieces of the Art of Tapestry from the Fourteenth to the Sixteenth Century*, New York, and the *Bulletin* of the Metropolitan Museum of Art. And further:
Holz, Edith. *Die Einhornjagd auf den Teppichen der Anne de Bretagne* (Unicorn Hunt in the Anne of Brittany Tapestries). Hamburg, 1967. The title poem of Anne Morrow Lindbergh's *The Unicorn and other Poems* relates to the final tapestry in the Cloisters collection.

The Cleveland series of tapestries *Allegorie de l'ephemere* (Allegory of the Ephemeris) is described in the just mentioned catalog of the magnificent exhibition *Chefs-d'oeuvre de la tapisserie* (Tapestry Masterpieces), held during the winter season 1973/1974 in the Grand Palais, Paris and subsequently in the Metropolitan Museum of Art, New York. That exhibition offered the unique opportunity for comparative viewing in two adjacent rooms of the two famous sets *La dame a la licorne* (The Lady on the Unicorn) from the Cluny Museum and the *Unicorn Tapestries* from the Cloisters. The catalog in question contains illustrations and descriptive particulars of all the works of art, as well as notes on the Cleveland tapestries.

The Living Unicorn

The 1830 Brockhaus (a noted German encyclopedia still in full swing) establishes that "contrary to Buffon, the existence of the unicorn is again a matter of credence." A skeptical view is found in: Rüppell, Eduard. *Reisen in Nubien, Kordofen und dem petraischen Arabien* (Travels in Nubia, Kordofan and Arabia Petra). Frankfurt am Main, 1829. 161 *et seq.*
Quests for unicorn sketches by bushmen in South African mountains, see Barrow, John. *An Account of Travels into the Interior of Southern Africa in the years 1797 and 1798*, vol. 1. London, 1801. 311 *et seq.* Also detailed discussion in the *Monthly Review*, vol. 35 (August 1901). 337 *et seq.*
Russel, John. *Tour in Germany*, 3rd ed. vol. 1. Edinburgh, 1825. 354 *et seq.;* describes a curious encounter with a Göttingen scholar who showed him a human skull with a single horn. It's difficult to determine which of them really came out best.
Fuhrmann, Ernst. *Das Tier in der Religion* (Animals in Religion). Munich, 1912. 27; takes it "for granted" that an animal did live in prehistoric Europe and Asia to which the descriptions in the legends apply, "that therefore the unicorn existed," without, unfortunately, furnishing any proof for that conviction. He does not state any sources at all by name, not even the "Chinese reports from most ancient times" from which it may definitely follow "that in some rare instances living specimens of such a unicorn had been found." On the realistic nature of the works of art, see:
Frey, Dagobert. *Kunstwissenschaftliche Grundfragen* (Fundamental Questions in Aesthetics). Vienna, 1946. I owe this important source as well as numerous other valuable suggestions to Professor Wolfgang Krönig of Cologne.
On the concept of the myth, the Karl Kerenyi Collection: *Die Eröffnung des Zugangs zum Mythos* (Opening Access to Myth). Darmstadt, 1967. Besides the editor's own contribution, there are also extracts from the writings of Bachofen, Creuzer, Herder, and Otto, and in addition, Schlegel's discourse.
On the unicorn myth alongside general or other literature, see: Brown, Robert. *The Unicorn, A Mythological Investigation*. London, 1881.

The unicorn in Shakespeare's works:
The Rape of Lucrece: "Time's glory is . . . To tame the unicorn and lion wild . . ."
The Tempest, III, 3, 22: "Now I will believe that there are unicorns . . ."
Timon of Athens, IV, 3, 339: "wert thou the unicorn pride and wrath would confound thee . . ."
Julius Caesar, II, 1, 204: "for he loves to hear that unicorns may be betray'd with trees . . ."

The hitherto misunderstood poem by Achim von Arnim was recognized by Friedrich Hoffman of Remagen. The latest edition of Arnim's novel *Die Kronenwächter* (The Regents), Munich: Hanser, 1974, has adopted the suggested amendment of the poem: *Einhorn* "Unicorn" instead of *Eichhorn* "Squirrel."

The unicorn myth was used somewhat coarsely in a novel: Buchanan, Thomas G. *The Unicorn*. New York: W. Sloane Associates, 1960. It serves as a symbolic trimming for many modern novels. Various authors are clearly well acquainted with the background. Martin Walser in the Suhrkamp publishing house organ *Dichten und Trachten* (Inspiration and Aspiration), no. 28 (1967), has written on the significance of the unicorn for his novel bearing its name as title. Without claiming to give a complete list, we may mention also Christian Giudicelli's *Le jeune homme à la licorne* (The Youth and the Unicorn), Paris, 1964; Iris Murdoch's *The Unicorn*. New York: Viking Press, 1963; Lotte Schalles's *Das Einhorn und die Löwen* (Unicorn and Lions), Cologne and Berlin, 1957; Martina Wied, *Das Einhorn* (The Unicorn), Vienna, 1948; Bertrand d'Astorg, *Le Mythe de la Dame à la Licorne* (The Lady and Unicorn Legend), Paris, 1963. In Peter S. Beagle's romance in verse *The Last Unicorn*, the holder of the title, whose downfall the reader attends, is a filly temporarily metamorphosed by magic into a woman. In *Les Dames à la Licorne,* Renè Barjavel and Olenka de Veer make a "real" unicorn the ancestress of a family of Irish temperament living at the present time. It is quite understandable that this prodigious animal should form a favorite subject for nursery tales.

See also:

Chancellor, R. D. *The Lady and the Unicorn* (Translation of a book by Verlet and Salet). London: Thames and Hudson, 1961.

Dinshaw, Vicalji. *The Unicorn*. CAMA Oriental Institute, Bombay (Journal no. 28 (1932), 97-100)

Edey, Marion. *The unicorn and other poems*. Brookville, Long Island; Brookville Press, *ca.* 1941.

Forbes, Rosita (Torr). *A unicorn in the Bahamas*. New York: Dutton, 1940.

Jones, Thomas Samuel. *The Unicorn and Other Sonnets*. Portland, Maine: Mosher Press, 1931.

Moure, Virginia. *The Unicorn: W. B. Yeats' Search for Reality*. New York: Macmillian, 1954.

Yeats, William Butler. *The Unicorn from the Stars*. In Collected Works. London, 1908.

Jorge Luis Borges and Margarita Guerrero have included our beast in their manual of whimsical zoology *Einhorn, Sphinx und Salamander* (Unicorn, Sphinx and Salamander), Munich, 1964.

Giancarlo Menotti's ballet "The Unicorn, the Gorgon, and the Manticore" has been musically reproduced by Angel Records on disc No. 35437. A merry arabesque, Sel Silverstein's Song "The Unicorn," deals with the animal's destruction in the Flood. (Recited, for example, by "The Irish Rovers," Decca Album DL 4951).

The Name Unicorn in Various Languages

In Old High German the animal was masculine *einhurno*, and also in Middle High German *einhurne* (see Grimm's famous Dictionary of the German Language), Grammatically it was more correct and more pleasant to say *der* Einhorn, plural die Einhorne, as in the popular ballads. But the usage *das* Einhorn, plural die Einhörner is now so deeply rooted that its extinction seems practically impossible. Grimm tells us also that in Anglo-Saxon the name of the beast was *ahyrne deor*. Louis Rzau: *Iconographie de l'Art Chretien*, Vol. 1, Paris 1955, pp. 89 *et seq.* collates the following denotations in various languages: Greek *monokeros,* Latin *unicornis,* Old French *lincorne,* Italian *unicorno* or *liocorno,* Spanish *unicornio,* English (of course) *unicorn* from the Latin, Russian *yedinorog*. He explains the modern French *licorne* as a sound-shift whereby *unicorne* was shortened to *nicorne*, the *n* dissimilating to *l* similarly to the way the word for orphan from the Latin *orphanus* first became *orphenin* and then transmuted to the current French *orphelin*.

Designating the animal's weapon as "the unicorn's horn" or even "unicorn horn" presents some difficulty since neither of these sound pleasing to the ear; the first appears to be the more usual. There is, however, a homonymous usage of "unicorn" also for the weapon as well as for the animal itself: Gryphius drinks "from gold and unicorn." Shepard gets round the problem quite neatly by calling the animal "unicorn" and its horn "alicorn" making use of an older Italian form *alicorna* (Portuguese *alicornio*). The piece in the Vienna Treasury (actually a narwhal's tusk) is formally called *ainkhorn*. This would be the not satisfactory form *Eingehorn* in High German, about as euphonious as "unikhorn" would be in English. Yet there must be some way round the problem. The huntsman calls the stag's branching horns its "antlers" and speaks of the number of "points." In German the term *Stangen* or points, gives the pleasant-sounding *Einhornstange*, in the singular and similarly in English we could surely adopt the equivalent "pike" which is "a weapon, a spike, and a sharp point" quite neatly for even if misheard the term "unicorn's pike" can sound only like "unicorn spike" which is to all intents and purposes the same thing and would cause no confusion.

202

Commentary on the Illustrations

The illustrations in this volume are arranged chiefly in groups according to their chronology and/or common subjects. Technical conditions, however, compelled departure from such order in some places. Our comparatively rich selection does not allow an exhaustive discussion of the whole multitude of unicorn portrayals. We can, nevertheless, give some pointers as to the places and motifs among which the animal may be looked for and found. Many discoveries still remain to be made by enthusiastic searchers.

The titles cited in the section "Unicorn Bibliography", especially those mentioned in the first part, generally contain some helpful further references to pictorial items. A large number of illustrations, especially from manuscripts, is carried in Father Jürgen W. Einhorn's book. The pictorial portion of Father Einhorn's book overlaps in only a few cases with the illustrations of the present volume which he expressly mentions as an iconographic reinforcement. We may also mention Guy de Tervarent's *Attributs et symboles dans l'art profane* 1450-1600 (Features and Symbols in Secular Art from Mid-Fifteenth Century Until the Beginning of the Seventeenth Century), vol. 2, Geneva, 1959. Fertile, encyclopedic sources on tapestries are Heinrich Göbel's *Wandteppiche* (Mural Hangings) in three parts, Leipzig, 1923-34, and Betty Kurth's *Die deutschen Bildteppiche des Mittelalters* (Medieval German Figured Tapestries), Vienna, 1926, and on the graphic arts, Albert Schramm's *Der Bilderdruck der Frühdrucke* (illuminations in Incunabula), and W.L. Schreiber's *Handbuch der Holz- und Metallschnitte des 15 Jb.* (Manual of Fifteenth Century Woodcuts and Metal Engravings), Berlin, 1891. From the numerous examples of unicorn symbols in iconography of the sixteenth and seventeenth centuries, Arthur Henkel and Albrecht Schoene have compiled a sumptuous volume *Emblemata*, Stuttgart, 1967, containing a selection which we have with due thanks used as one of our sources. The bibliographic references which we give for individual illustrations in the following list are intended to guide the reader in his own further researches and not to be exhaustive.

Frontispiece: Schiller's coat of arms, from the Schiller National Museum, Marbach.

1. Unicorn (Ibex) from North Persia, dating from middle of second century B.C. Three inches tall. Dr. B. Sprengel's collection, Hannover. Catalog *Seven Hundred Years of Art in Iran*, Essen, 1962. (No. 65 in catalog).
Photo by Hans Wagner, Hannover.

2. Virgin and unicorn from *Hortus sanitatis*, Mainz, 1491.

3. Start of chapter from Walther Ryff's German edition of Albertus Magnus's bestiary, Frankfurt, 1545. Albert lived from approximately 1193 until 1280; the date of his original manuscript is controversial.

4. By J. Collaert (1545-1622?) after J. van der Straet or Stradanus (1523-1605). Unicorn Hunt in India. The City of Antwerp Gallery of Copperplate Engravings which possesses a complete set, has been kind enough to advise us that this is one of a series of 104 engravings of hunting scenes and animal fights issued by Jan Galle (undated). Van der Straet worked a long time in Italy and drafted many cartoons for the Gobelin tapestries. The caption indicates that the Indian unicorn hunt proceeded with the king's permission and mentions also the medical use of the horn.
Holstein, F. W., *Dutch and Flemish Etchings*, vol. 4 on Collaert; von Wurzbach, A., Niederl, *Künstlerlexikon* (Netherlands Art Lexicon), vol. 2 on Stradanus (van der Straet).

5. Dispute between the quadrupeds and the birds. Woodcut by Johann Zainer, from Aesop's Fables printed in Ulm, *ca.* 1476.

6. The Unicorn in Paradise, from Johann Joachim Becher's *Parnassus Illustratus Medicinalis,* Ulm, 1663. The text enumerates the parts (and secretions) of the human body which are medically serviceable. The work also contains an equivalent section on the unicorn, the picture of which is less informative iconographically. Compare illustration 57.

7/8. Wild Men on unicorn hunt. Franconian woven tapestry *ca.* 1450. "The wild man with the lover's knot round his head slays the unicorn in the damsel's lap. The unicorn is current as a religious allegory. In this particular secular version, the hunter embodies lust, and concupiscence; the mythical beast represents pure love or virtue." From the catalog *Medieval Wild Men*, Hamburg, 1963, 42. Regarding religious variants, see illustration 47, for example.
Photo courtesy of Bavarian National Museum, Munich

9. Miniature from a manuscript in the possession of the British Museum (Harley 4751). The Latin text depends on the description in Megasthenes and/or Aelian. Photo Courtesy of British Museum, London

10. Tapestry of the Creation, centerpiece *ca.* eleventh or twelfth century from Gerona Cathedral, Spain. The sector to the right beneath the center shows Adam naming the animals, at which time there was as yet no mate for him among the creatures present (*cf.* Genesis 2: 19, 20). This scene was frequently depicted in early Christian miniatures right down through to Baroque tapestries. **See Pedro del Palol and Max Hirmer's** *Spanien, Kunst des frühen Mittelalters* (Spain – Early Medieval Art), 1965, 126 *et seq.*
Photo by MAS, Barcelone (Spain)

11. Virgin and unicorn in miniature from Byzantine Khludov Psalter of ninth–century production and used in the Hagia Sophia. Now in the Historical Museum, Moscow.
Ebersolt, Jan. *La Miniature byzantine*, Paris, 1926;
Dufrenne, S. "Psautiers byzantins." In *L'Oeil* no. 167 (November 1968).

12. The Virgin Mary suckles her child, *Christ the Unicorn.*
Miniature from the Pantocrator psalter, ninth century, Byzantine Pantocrator Cloister on Mount Athos.
Dufrenne, S. (see under 11); Miss Dufrenne was kind enough to obtain the photo for us.
Huber, Paul, *Athos – Leben, Glaube, Kunst* (Mount Athos: Its Life Belief, and Art), 1969.

13. Opening miniature to St. Matthew's Gospel in the Averbode Book of the Four Gospels, mid-twelfth century. University Library, Liège. Next to the Evangelist are the Virgin Mary with the unicorn, and Job to whom the voice of the Lord is saying "Will the unicorn be willing to serve thee or abide by thy crib? Canst thou bind the unicorn with his band in the furrow? or will he harrow the valleys after thee?" (Job 39:– 9, 10), while Mary holds the subdued unicorn in her lap. Rosalie B. Green in *De Artibus opuscula XL* (Jubilee volume for Panokfsky), 157 *et seq.*
Photo from Foto Marburg

14. Sixth or seventh century unicorn relief from choirstall in San Saba, Aventine Hill, Rome. Wehrhahn-Stauch in RDK suggests that in this case the unicorn 'has a rather secular meaning, since it accompanies reliefs of a stag and of a horseman with falcon.' Nevertheless this seems to be the oldest representation of a unicorn within the precincts of a Christian church.
Photo by Dr. Edelgard Meyer-Landrut, Meerbusch

15. The so-called pastoral staff of St. Boniface, from about the first half of the thirteenth century. Probably of Sicilian origin.
von Falke, Otto, "Ein Bischofstab islamischer Arbeit und seine Verwandten" (A Pastoral Staff of Moslem Workmanship and its Analogs), In *Pantheon* vol. 7 (1935).   Photo by Retzlaff

16. Pillar (fragment) with mythical beasts, from the former Cluniac Monastery of Souvigny (Allier Department, France), twelfth century. The other faces of the pillar show people from foreign nations, the zodiac and the monthly tasks. The unicorn between the griffin and the elephant, with its muzzle ready open for roaring and its curly tail, seems to follow the lines described by Megasthenes and Aelian; its horn is broken off halfway.
Mâle. *L'art religieux de XII^c siecle en France* (Twelfth century French Religious Art) (fifth ed. 1947), 323 *et seq.*
Photo by Giraudon, Paris

17. Miniature to Psalm 22 (21) in the Stuttgart psalter, France, early **ninth century. Württemberg State Library, Stuttgart. The** Crucifixion (in which Christ is uttering the first words of that psalm, "My God, my God, why hast thou forsaken me?"); the lion and unicorn which are mentioned in the psalm as dangerous animals, and below them the division of Christ's raiment. Facsimile edition with extra volume of scientific researches (Stuttgart, 1968)
Photo from Foto Marburg

18. Baptismal font in Freudenstadt Town Church, brought there from some other Black Forest church. *Ca.* eleventh century, new red sandstone.
von Blankenburg, Vera, *Heilige und dämonische Tiere* (Sacred and Demoniac Animals), Leipzig, 1943.
Keppler, Eugen, "Das Bildwerk des Taufsteins in Freudenstadt" **(The Imagery on the Freudenstadt Font). In** *Archiv für christliche Kunst,* vol. 7 (1889).
Schade, Herbert, *Dämonen und Monstren* **(Demons and Monsters).** Regensburg, 1962.
Photo from Württemberg Provincial Sculptuary Center, Landesbildstelle Württemberg, Stuttgart.

19. Daniel's vision (Daniel 8). The goat with one notable horn (Alexander) overthrows the arrogant two-horned ram (the kings of Media and Persia), and from his head four new horns came up (the realms of the Diadochi). Friar Obeco's miniature completed 970 in the Valcavado Abbey eastward of León. In the Library of Holy Cross College, Valladolid. The Daniel commentary was frequently written, also with miniatures, as an appendix to a text by St. Beatus of Liébana in the tenth century in Spain, since apocalyptic visions in the age of the conflict with the Moors and in the light of the imminent approach of the year 1000 clearly correspond to a then-current frame of mind. One of these manuscripts is in facsimile print with explanatory comments which also appear to enter into Obeco's transcript:
Sancti Beati a Liebana in Apocalypsium Codex Gerundiensis (Of the Blessed Saint of Liebana in the Gerona Codex Apocalypse), (Olten and Lausanne, 1961)   Photo by MAS, Barcelona

20/21. Mosaic floor in Otranto Cathedral, completed by Friar Pantaleone *ca.* 1165. Illustration 21 shows detail of medallion representing a unicorn with monk (Pantaleone?). The coy priest is occupying to some extent the stance normally taken by the Virgin; he is gentling the unicorn. The gigantic mosaic, of which our illustration shows only the minor portion at the intersection of the nave, contains altogether a whole mythological bestiary in figures of diverse origin.

Finsler, Hans, "Pantaleone's Mosaic in Otranto". In *Du/Atlantis* (October 1965). Numerous excellent illustrations.
Gianfreda, Grazio, *Il mosaico pavimentale della basilica cattedrale di* **Otranto (The Mosaic Flooring in the Cathedral Basilica of Otranto).** Casamari Abbey Printing House, Frosinone 1965. Also profusely illustrated.
Photo from Zurich School of Applied Arts

22. Arabian ivory casket. Detail with two winged unicorns from Pamplona Cathedral, Spain, 1005. See Richard Ettinghausen, "The Unicorn". In *Studies in Moslem Iconography* (Washington, 1950). He says these are the earliest representations of the unicorn iconography in Muslim art so far traced.
Photo by MAS, Barcelona

23. The so-called Holzkirchen Horseman. Dedicatory stone from the former monastery church at Holzkirchen in the Spessart region, *ca.* 1100; of new red sandstone. On demolition of the romanesque monastery in 1729, it was transferred to an outside wall of the small modern residence (by Balthasar Neumann), and taken inside in 1931. There is a hole in the center, which may in its time have served as channel for a fountain outlet pipe. The inscription reads AEQUESTER AEDIBUS IN-(OST)-RIS SIT T TUA DEXTERA XRE (As thou ridest O Christ, let thy right hand rest on our dwelling). The Holzkirchen Benedictine monastery was founded in 775 by Count Troandus of the Waldsass province and ceded to Charlemagne with surrounding real estate. The emperor **in his turn presented the property to Fulda monastery, the foundation of St. Boniface,** *Die Künstdenkmäler des Königreiches Bayern* (Artistic Landmarks of the Kingdom of Bavaria), vol. 3, no. 7. Marktheidenfeld Local Government, 1912.
Photo by Gundermann, Würzburg

24. Twelfth century unicorn relief from Notre Dame de la Règle abbey, in the Adrien Dubouché Museum, Limoges (Upper Vienne).
Photo Courtesy of Archives Photographiques, Paris

25. Antependium (altar frontal) with sacred beasts, from a Swiss Maurist church, *ca.* 1300. In Thun castle museum. (Part of the animal iconography, an early twentieth-century copy, is a wall hanging in Chillon castle on Lake Geneva). In addition to the unicorn, the medallions depict the four symbols of the gospels, as well as a cock, a panther, an ostrich, a ram, a phoenix, a pelican, and a stag. No satisfactory explanation appears to have been found yet for the emanation from the unicorn's muzzle which sweeps like a flame upward over the animal.
Gressky, Wolfgang, "Das Einhorn vom Medaillonteppich im Thuner Schlossmuseum und andere Schweizer Einhorn-Darstellungen" (The unicorn from the medaillion tapestry in Thun castle museum, and other unicorn iconography). In 1968 *Annual Report of the Thun Historical Museum.*
Photo by Meier Photos, Thun

26. Chest front, Westphalia, *ca.* 1300. Berlin Public Museum (Köpenick Castle Museum of Applied Arts).
Schade, Günther, *Deutsche Möbel aus sieben Jahrhunderten* **(Seven** Centuries of German Furnishings), Leipzig, n.d.
Photo Courtesy of German National Museums, Berlin.

27. Virgin and unicorn. Detail from the so-called Malterer (the name of the donors) tapestry in the Augustine Museum, 1310-29. At Freiburg (Breisgau). This is a long fabric to be spread on a wall behind a bench, and comprises several examples of the favorite subject of 'feminine wiles'. Whether the capture of the unicorn by the damsel should be counted among these womanly wiles, or whether the intention is to show the counterpart of heavenly love **is somewhat controversial. Evidence for the second interpretation is that the piece comes from the Adelshausen cloister estate.**
Photo from Karl Alber Publications, Freiburg in Breisgau

28. Young unicorn. India ink sketch to Psalm 28 (29) in the Utrecht psalter, early ninth century. According to the text of the psalm, this is a young, gambolling unicorn, which here, skipping headlong as the wind, has run its horn fast into a tree trunk. The Utrecht psalter, currently in Utrecht University Library, is considered the most important and earliest product of the Reims school of painting. It contains still a few further unicorn pictures
Baum, Julius, *Die Malerei und Plastik des Mittelalters* (Medieval Painting and sculpture), vol. 2 Germany, France and Britain (1933)
de Wald, E. T. *The Illustrations of the Utrecht Psalter.* Princeton, New Jersey, 1933.

29. Unicorn caught headlong in a tree. Chairhead in refectory of Praglia Abbey near Padua, Italy, 1726, with motto reading *Praeproperum poenitet* (Rash haste brings speedy woe). The illustrated guide to the abbey contains photos of thirty-six similar chair decorations, many with animal likenesses.

30. **Tobias Stimmer. The unicorn couple refuses to enter Noah's ark. Woodcut in** *Neue künstliche Figuren Biblischer Historien* **(Modern art figures from Biblical history), Basel, 1576.**
Photo Courtesy of Bavarian State Library, Munich

31. Abbot Ratgar of Fulda as a rampageous unicorn. Copper engraving in Christopher Brouwer's *Fuldensium antiquitatum libri III* (Antiquities of Fulda, Book Three), Antwerp, 1612, after a lost ninth-century miniature. The unicorn also appears in other connotations as a symbol for Fulda Monastery. Compare Illustration 23. **Gerstenberg, Kurt,** *Die deutschen Baumeisterbilder des Mittelalters* (German Medieval Master Builders' Portraits), Berlin, **1966. Simson, Bernhard,** *Jahrbücher des Fränkischen Reiches unter Ludwig dem Frommen* (Annals of the Franconian Kingdom under Louis the Pious), 1874.

32. Seizure of the unicorn, from the Bern *Physiologus*, ninth century.

33. The water-detoxifying unicorn as symbol for the dictum *Victrix casta fides* ("Pure faith overcomes"). In Nicolas Reusner's *Emblemata*, 1584, vol. 2, no. 4 (Henkel and Schoene), col. 421.

34. The unicorn subdued, as symbol for the saying *Hoc virtutis amor* ("This is the love of virtue"). In Joachim Camerarius' *Symbolorum et emblematum centuria altera* (Signs and Symbols of Past Ages), 1595, no. 12 (Henkel and Schoene), col. 422.

35. A page from the *Defensorium inviolatae virginitatus Mariae* (Compurgation of the Unsullied Virginity of Mary); woodcut probably from late fifteenth century. In other editions Francis of Resza (from Retz on the Enns), professor in Vienna, is named as the author. This particular edition was printed in Saragossa though not with woodcuts necessarily of Spanish origin. The pictures on the page reproduced here show Xerxes whose wine turns to blood in the goblet, the bird Bonafa who copulated by kissing, the transformation of river water into blood at Toulouse, and the taming of the unicorn by the virgin – all miracles intended to prove the feasibility of supernatural events. ("If the unicorn bows before the virgin, why then should not a Virgin bring the Word of God into the world.") Facsimile edition with commentary by W. L. Schreiber, 1910.

36. Virgin with unicorn, fifteenth-century cushion cover from Cologne. In the Schnütgen Museum, Cologne. Included in the catalog *Herbst des Mittelalters* (Harvest of the Middle Ages), Cologne, 1970, no. 453.
Photo from Rheinisches Bildarchiv, Cologne

37. Painted Romance beam, fourteenth to fifteenth century from Barcelona. Illustration from the journal *Humboldt*, 1970, no. 41.
Photo from MAS, Barcelona

38. Tibetan unicorn, seventeenth century, sixteen inches long. In the Heydt Collection, Rietberg Museum, Zurich. The unicorn (the gazelle of the Buddha legend) kneels on its forelegs, to listen devoutly to the Master's words in his first sermon. Here, the horn between the ears stands as a symbol of Nirvana.
Photo by Hans Finsler courtesy of Rietberg Museum, Zurich.

39. Unicorn and elephant. Top portion of thirteenth to fourteenth century scriptural tile from Iran. In the Islamic Museum, East Berlin. As the elephant is provided with a decorative saddle, it is reasonable to assume that the unicorn is not driving him forward as a prize of battle, but that the elephant is luring the unicorn into captivity, as they do also with wild elephants. The tile is in two colors (blue and brown).
See Ettinghausen, "The Unicorn." *Studies in Muslim Iconography.* Washington, 1950, plate 16.
Photo courtesy of Berlin State Museum

40. Shadhahvar: miniature from a late fourteenth century Iraki manuscript in private ownership. This type of unicorn has forty-two holes in its horn, through which the wind produces an enchanting melody. This first appears in literature in 900 B..C Cf. Ettinghausen, *op. cit.*, plate 42.

41. Iskandar (Alexander the Great) fighting the carcadann, the classic form of Moslem unicorn (cf. Megasthenes' cartazoon). Manuscript from the Persian *Shakh-Namah* (Catalog of Kings), coe 1320. In Museum of Fine Arts, Boston. Cf. Ettinghausen, *op. cit.*
Photo courtesy of Museum of Fine Arts, Boston.

42. Horseman fighting unicorn. Cap of a twelfth century Iraki storage pitcher. In the Islamic Art Museum of the Prussian Cultural Heritage Foundation, West Berlin. Ettinghausen, *op. cit.* **Photo by Walter Steinkopf, from Prussian Cultura! Heritage,** Foundation, Berlin.

43. The slaying of the unicorn. Miniature from a medieval manuscript in the British Museum .
Photo courtesy of British Museum, London

44. French ivory casket from first half of the fourteenth century, showing unicorn hunt on right and a scene from *Tristan and Isolde* on left. Caskets of this kind, in which the erotic nature of the equivocal story of the unicorn hunt prevails were manufactured on the large scale in France. A similar item is in the strong room of Wawel Castle, Cracow. See Johann von Antoniewicz's *Ikono-*

graphisches zu Chrestien de Troyes (Iconography on Chretien of Troyes, twelfth century poet of the Grail legend), Romanische Forschungen (Romance Researches), vol. 5, 1889.
Photo courtesy of British Museum, London

45. Slaying of the unicorn. Miniature from an Italian bestiary manuscript ca. thirteenth to fourteenth century.
Photo courtesy of British Museum, London

46. Enameled silver tray showing death of unicorn. Rhenish workmanship, ca. 1330. The scene is generally given a secular interpretation by connoisseurs. The black-and-white enlargement shows the unusual graphic quality of the heavily colored work of art which is only about three inches in diameter.
Photo courtesy of Bavarian National Museum, Munich

47. The martyrdom of the unicorn. Quatrefoil in choirstall in Cologne cathedral. Early fourteenth century.
Photo from Rheinische Bildarchiv, Cologne

48. The martyrdom of the unicorn. Misericord in choirstall of Trinity Church, Stratford-on-Avon.

49. Pisanello (Antonio Pisano, ca. 1395 to 1451/55 ?). Bronze medal to Cecilia Gonzaga. Reverse (The obverse shows Cecilia's portrait). Mantua, 1447. Pisanello is deemed the creator of medal engraving. The one we illustrate is regarded as one of his finest productions. The design combines various symbols of chastity in honor of a member of the reigning family of Mantua. See Franco Panvini Rosati's German language catalog of Italian Medals and Plaquettes, 1966.
Photo from Berlin State Museum

50. Pisanello (see no. 49 above). Innocence protects the unicorn from the huntsmen. Uffizi Palace Gallery, Florence.
Photo by Anderson, Rome.

51. Fight with the unicorn. Detail from a frieze in Strassburg Minster. **The middle portion of the lance, with which the man is** attacking the rearing unicorn, has broken off.
Photo courtesy of Oeuvre de Notre Dame, Strassburg.

52. Wild man fighting unicorn. Detail from a wall hanging, Strassburg ca. 1400. In Boston Fine Arts Museum, Charles Potter Kling Fund. Major, Emil. *Strassburger Bilderteppiche aus gotischer Zeit* (Gothic Period Pictorial Tapestries from Strassburg). Basel, no date.
Photo courtesy of Museum of Fine Arts, Boston.

53. **Unicorn on wall bracket in St. Vitus' Cathedral, Prague.** Fourteenth century.
Photo from Foto Marburg.

54. Unicorn in floor mosaic from church of St. John the Evangelist, Ravenna, thirteenth century.
Photo by Giraudon, Paris.

55. Unicorn on north portal of the spine of St. Philip and Jacob, **Altötting (Bavaria). Early sixteenth century. (Surrounding this** portion are other symbolic animal figures relating to the virginity of Mary).
Photo from Altötting District Photo Center (Seitz).

56. Annunciation. Detail from the Göss antependium, embroidered altar frontal ca. 1240. Austrian Museum of Applied Art, Vienna. This antependium is a component of an extensive set of communion vestments, on the other portions of which the unicorn also appears many times. The antependium bears the inscription (CHUNEG(UNDIS) ABBA(TISSA) ME FEC (IT) ("Abbess Gunigund made me"). The encircling inscription is Gabriel's greeting "AVE MARIA GRACIA PLENA DOMINUS TECU(M) **BENEDICTA TU" ("Hail Mary with thee is the full grace of God, Blessed art thou").** Dreger, Moritz. "Das Gösser Ornat" article on the Göss vestments in *Kunst und Kunsthandwerk*, vol. II 1908).
Photo from Austrian Museum for Applied Art, Vienna.

57. **Early sixteenth-century Swiss Garden-of-Eden rug. Prussian Cultural Heritage Foundation, Applied Art Museum, Berlin. The unicorn after the Fall of Man as sign of future redemption. The Lord calls from the heights of heaven. "Adam, where art thou?"
Photo from National Museum of Prussian Cultural Heritage, Applied Art Museum, Berlin.**

58. Cardunn. Drawing after a thirteenth century Iraki manuscript in the British Museum. Ettinghausen, *op. cit.* plate 7.

59. Boetius A. Bolswerth (1580-1633). *The Man in the Well*, copper engraving. With regard to the legend on which this allegory rests, **see Vetter, Ewald M. *Media vita* in *Gesammelte Aufsätze zur Kulturgeschichte Spaniens*** (Collected Essays on the Cultural History of Spain), Münster, 1960.
Photo from Prentenkabinet R. U., Leyden.

60. **Winged unicorn from a gilt-enameled Syrian glass receptacle**

ca. 1330-1340. Detail drawing. Freer Gallery of Art. Washington. Ettinghausen, *op. cit.* plates 1 and 2.

61, 62. Three different types of unicorn, from Jonston Johannes. *Theatrum universale omnium animalium* (Panorama of All Animals), Heilbronn, 1755.

63. Water unicorn from the painted ceiling of the Church of St. Martin at Zillis in the Grisons, ca. first half of the twelfth century. The water unicorn here shown is part of a frieze of demonic sea creatures in the ocean surrounding the solid earth. Murbach, Ernst and Hansen, Peter. *Zillis: Die romanische Bilderdecke der Kirche St. Martin* (The Painted Ceiling of St. Martin's Church, Zillis), Zürich, 1967.
Photo by Boissonas, Geneva.

64. Detail from a shrine altar to the Virgin Mary, ca. first third of the fifteenth century. In Bonn Provincial Museum (formerly in the no longer existent Cologne church of St. Mary on the stairway to the cathedral). The inscription around the picture of the Virgin and unicorn gives the iconographic elucidation of the scene: *Unicorn sum significoque deum, virgineis digitis tangendo fit hec fera mitis* ("I am the unicorn and a sign for God. The wild beast is tamed by the touch of a virgin's fingers").
Photo from Rheinisches Bildarchiv, Cologne.

65. Virgin and unicorn. Side of pew in choirstall of Maulbronn monastery church, latter half of fifteenth century.
Photo from Württemberg Provincial Photographic Center, Stuttgart.

66. Virgin and unicorn. Medallion on the high altar of the former monastery church of Cismar, early fourteenth century.
Photo by W. Castelli, Lübeck.

67. Virgin and unicorn on Marian pectoral painted on portion of cathedral dome by Stephan Lochner (died 1451). A similar adornment is worn by the Virgin in the picture *Maria in der Rosenlaube* (Mary in the Rose Arbor), Wallraf-Richartz Museum, Cologne.
Photo from Rheinisches Bildarchiv, Cologne.

68. Virgin and unicorn on keystone from St. Stephan's church, Vienna, before 1340. During battle actions of World War Two, this stone was badly damaged and has been replaced by a copy in the structure.
Photo from Austrian Office of Federal Monuments, Vienna.

69, 70. Wild woman and unicorn (cf. illustration 80) on side of pew in Our Lady's Minster choirstall, Konstanz. Illustration 70 is a section from the opposite side of the pew, showing the wild woman caught in a thicket and menaced by canine demons. The sequence must therefore be looked at in reverse: Entanglement in sin and subsequent redemption.
Photo by Alfons Rettich, Konstanz.

71. Miniature. Christmas scene with Marian symbols from the Stammheim missal of presbyter Henricus of Neidel, mid-twelfth century, in the possession of Baron Fürstenberg. Indications to the virginity of Mary are to be found *inter alia* in the lower portion of the icon, namely Gideon and his fleece, the shut gate (mentioned by the prophet Ezekiel: *Porta hec clausa erit*—Ezekiel 44:2 "This gate shall be shut . . ."), and the unicorn.
Beissel, Stephan. "Ein Missale aus Hildesheim und die Anfänge der Armenbibel" (A Missal from Hildesheim and the Beginnings of the Charity Bible). In *Zeitschrift für christliche Kunst,* vol. 15, (1902); *Weltkunst aus Privatbesitz* (International Art in Private Ownership) Catalog, Cologne, 1968.
Photo from Rheinisches Bildarchiv, Cologne.

72. Mystic unicorn hunt in the *Hortus conclusus,* Lower Rhineland woven tapestry circa 1500. The conversation between Gabriel and Mary is repeated on the lettered strips.
Photo courtesy of Bavarian National Museum, Munich.

73. Unicorn hunt. Center panel of an altar in St. Mary's Cathedral, Erfurt, ca. 1420. One of the earliest presentations of the subject. In addition to the chief characters, the *Hortus conclusus* contains a number of female saints and the Blessed Maurice. Vetter, Ewald M. *Maria im Rosenhag* (Mary in the Rose Enclosure). Düsseldorf, 1956.
Photo from Deutsche Fotothek (German Photo Library), Dresden (Möbius).

74. Giovanni Maria Falconetto, ca. 1458 to ca. 1540. Unicorn hunt. Fresco in church of St. Peter the Martyr, Verona. Left of the section shown here is the scene of Gabriel with the hounds. On the right, outside of the *hortus conclusus,* is Gideon. An ostrich leaving its eggs to hatch in the sun comes into this picture as a customary symbol of salvation.
Photo by Alinari, Florence.

75. Unicorn hunt. Fresco in the city Church of Our Lady at Memmingen, (Bavaria) circa 1460-1470.
Photo by Lala Aufsberg, Sonthofen.

76. Basel tapestry with symbolic animals, ca. 1480. On the motto strip for the unicorn: *Got muos al geschaffen hahn* ("God certainly created all things"). The other animals are the boar for ferocity,

the lion for strength, and the stag for yearning toward God. Lanz, Hans. *Gotische Bildteppiche* (Gothic Figured Tapestries). Bern, 1955. Photo from Historical Museum, Basel.

77. Feminine cunning on capital of a column from the Church of St. Peter in Caen, France. Virgil in the basket, and a unicorn hunt. Photo by Giraudon, Paris.

78. Damsel with unicorn. Detail from a Basel tapestry with symbolic animals, fifteenth century. The Basel Historical Museum contains a collection of seventeen superb gothic figured tapestries, including a dozen of Basel workmanship, on which the unicorn appears several times. This one dating from the time of the Council of Basel 1431-1448 "from its sumptuousness gives the impression that the patron who commissioned it must have been a person of great consequence." (Lanz *op. cit.*)
Photo from Historical Museum, Basel.

79. Rhenish trinket box from latter half of the fifteenth century. Wild hunters in the forest, one of whom is leading the unicorn carrying the queen of the savages. The other sides of the box (which "belongs among the most exquisite late Gothic trinket caskets known to us,") are further scenes from the life of the wild people. The unicorn appears frequently as an erotic allegory on such caskets. "Die wilden Leute im Mittelalter" (Wild Folk in the Middle Ages) catalog, Hamburg 1963. Kohlhaussen, Heinrich. *Minnekästchen im Mittelalter* (Trinket boxes in the Middle Ages). Berlin, 1928.
Photo courtesy of History of Art Museum, Vienna.

80. Female savage with unicorn. Late fifteenth century Strassburg tapestry (chairback cover). Cf. illustration 69. Emil Major, *op. cit.*
Photo courtesy of Historical Museum, Basel.

81. Wild man and wild woman in the *hortus conclusus*, Gobelin tapestry from south Holland ca. 1500 to 1510, from a series of Wild Man or Indian scenes (kindly communication from Louise E. Erkelens, Sectional Superintendent, Rijksmuseum, Amsterdam). Photo from Netherlands National Museum, Amsterdam.

82. Virgin and unicorn from an edition of the *Defensorium virginitatis* (cf. illustration 35) ascribed to Francis of Retz, at Ysenhut, Basel, ca. 1490.

83. Virgin and unicorn. Seventeenth-century Spanish woodcut. Agustin Durán y Sanpere's volume on Spain (in German) in *Populäre Druckgraphik Europas* (Graphical Printings of the Nations of Europe). Munich, 1971.

84. Erhard Reuwich, woodcut of Animals in the Holy Land for Bernhard von Breydenbach's *Reise ins Heilige Land* (Journey to the Holy Land), Mainz, 1486.

85. Antependium with unicorn hunt (detail). Late fifteenth century. In St. Mary's church, Gelnhausen.
Photo from German Art publishing house Deutscher Kunstverlag, Munich. Copyright by Gelnhausen Protestant Congregation.

86. Pope and unicorn, miniature from the so-called papal prophecies in a fifteenth- to sixteenth-century Latin manuscript. These widely distributed and long respected "prophecies" are not prophecies and have no connection whatever with the Sicilian pope di Fiore to whom they have been ascribed. They relate partly to events preceding their appearances somewhere about the late fourteenth century, partly to the equally apocryphal Byzantine predictions which were ascribed to the (ninth century) emperor Leo the Wise. From these Leonine predictions the unicorn also passed over into the "papal prophecies" and was next connected with Pope Honorius IV and later with Gregory XII. The texts are largely "meaningless gibberish" (Grundmann). Grundmann, Herbert. "Die Pabstprophetien des Mittelalters" (The Medieval Papal Prophecies), *Archiv für Kulturgeschichte*, vol. 19, Pt. 1. On the Byzantine predictions, see Bousset, Wilhelm. "Beiträge zur Geschichte der Eschatologie" (Contributions to the History of Eschatology), *Zeitschrift fur Kirchengeschichte*, vol. 20, 1900.
Photo from Bavarian National Library, Munich.

87. Detail from pictorial sheet of *The Quadrupeds*, eighteenth century Spanish woodcut. Agustin Durán y Sanpere, *op. cit.*

88. Unicorn skeleton reconstructed by Otto von Guericke from fossils found in the Sewecke Mountains limestone quarries near Quedlinburg (1663) and reproduced in Leibnitz' posthumous work on the origin of the earth *Protogaea*.

89. Official form of British coat of arms as used by Her Majesty's Stationery Office. At the death of Queen Elizabeth I in 1603, the crown of England passed to the House of Stuart, who brought the Scottish unicorn over to accompany the English lion as supporter for the crest. The crest of Scotland still retains two unicorns as supporters, but how the unicorn came to enter the Scottish device is obscure.
London, H. Stanford. Royal Beasts, 1956.

90. Hans Baldung, called Grien. Crest of the Baldung family (see also jacket of this book). The crest dates probably from the 1520s. This family crest appears also on the tombstone of Hans Baldung's daughter-in-law by the portal of Lichtenthal Mon-

astery. Church near Baden-Baden. Hans Baldung Grien catalog.
Karlsruhe, 1959.
Photo by Foto Marburg.

91-96. The Lady with the Unicorn, collection of Gobelin tapestries ca. 1500, now in Cluny Museum, Paris.
Photo courtesy of Cluny Museum, Paris.

97. Lukas Kilian (1579-1637). Satirical allegory on the papacy, aquarelle. A warrior carrying the torch of truth, and a lion as symbol of strength bar the way to the Pope, who is travelling arrogantly in the unicorn chariot after the style of the *Trionfi* of noble ladies of the Renaissance.
"Augsburger Barock" catalog, Augsburg, 1968.
Photo from Germanic National Museum, Nürnberg.

98. Lady and unicorn. Relief in Castel Sant' Angelo, Rome. Library Hall decoration from the time of Pope Paul III (1634-1549).
Motto *Cedo alla purezza* ("I yield to purity").
Photo by Anderson, Rome.

99. Piero della Francesca (died 1492). Triumph of Battista Sforza, Duchess of Urbino. In the Uffizi Palace, Florence.
Photo by Alinari, Florence.

100. Giorgione (ca. 1478-1510). Lady with unicorn as an allegory of chastity, Rijksmuseum, Amsterdam.
Photo from Rijksmuseum, Amsterdam.

101. Lady with unicorn. Fresco in Castel Sant' Angelo, Rome, ascribed to Perino del Vaga (1501 to 1547), who during his final years was admittedly working in the castle with twenty-eight (!) assistants.
Photo by Alinari, Florence.

102. Bernardino Luini (ca. 1480-1532), Procris and the unicorn. Fresco in the National Gallery of Art, Washington, Samuel H Kress Collection. The unicorn is not spoken of in the ancient mythology and literature (Ovid, *Metamorphoses*, Book VIII). Relating to Procris: Here we are probably dealing with some Renaissance extension.
Photo from National Gallery of Art, Washington.

103. Female rider on unicorn (Debauchery?). Spandrelfiller in the church of Our Lady at Hal (Belgium), ca. 1400.
Photo by Foto Marburg.

104. Immodesty versus virginal Modesty and Chastity. Broadsheet from last quarter of the fifteenth century, Albertina, Vienna. Virtue rides a unicorn and her shield bears an angel; Vice rides a bear and her scutcheon is a hog. Haberditzl, Franz Martin. *Die Einblattdrucke des XV. Jahrhunderts in der Kupferstichsammlung der Hofbibliothek zu Wien* (Fifteenth century printed broadsheets in the Vienna Court Library copperplate engravings collection, 1920.
Photo by Albertina, Vienna.

105 **François Clouet (ca. 1522-1572), Diane de Poitiers, National Gallery of Art, Samuel H. Kress Collection, Washington. Diane was the mistress of the immature king** Henry II of France, and she exerted strong influence in the political sense. In the portrait which shows her and her children with their wetnurse, the court painter has introduced the unicorn discreetly on the chairback in the background as a symbol of virtue.
Photo from National Gallery of Art, Washington.

106. Hans Valkenauer, Crest of the Marx von Nussdorf family, ca. 1478. Detail from tombstone in the collegiate church at Laufen on the Salzach. The stone is of red marble.
Photo by Lala Aufsberg, Sonthofen.

107. Arms of the Knesebeck family, on bronze font in Ratzeburg cathedral, 1440.
Photo by W. Castelli, Lübeck.

108. Unicorn tympanum, Montferrand Wards, Clermont-Ferrand. Photo: Archives Photographiques, Paris. (A copy is in the Cloisters, New York.)

109. Seal of the city of Gmünd in Swabia, 1319.
Photo by Foto Schweizer, Schwäbisch-Gmünd.

110. Bracteate (coin with device stamped through silver foil on one side), Bludenz, ca. 1260. Diameter $\frac{3}{4}$ inch. The city of Bludenz in the lower Arlberg range (Vorarlberg/Austria) bears a unicorn in the coat of arms.

111. Hans Holbein the Younger (ca. 1498-1543). Casement sketch (heraldic design) with unicorns, colorwashed Indian ink drawing. Photo from Copper Engravings Collection of the Public Art Collections, Basel.

112. Garden of Eden. Detail from private altar of Duke Albert V, Court Workshops of Munich, 1573–1574.
Lieb, Norbert. *München–Die Geschichte seiner Kunst* (Munich—the History of its Art), Munich, 1971.

113. Side of pew from Salzburg Cathedral. (Every alternate pew has the unicorn decoration).
Photo from Landesbildstelle (Provincial Pictorial Center), Salzburg.

114. Lucas Cranach the Elder (1472-1553). Group of animals. Detail from Garden of Eden scene. National Art Collections, Dresden.
Photo by Deutsche Fotothek, Dresden.

115/116. Sacraments of Confirmation and Ordination. Detail from baptismal font dated 1499 in Municipal Church (formerly St. Mary's) in Reutlingen. The unicorn otherwise and elsewhere frequently coordinated with the patroness saint of the church appears here as evidence for masculine "purity."
Photo from Landesbildstelle, Württemberg, Stuttgart.

117. Altar to the Virgin Mary, with mystic unicorn hunt, 1506, from Lübeck cathedral (formerly dedicated to the Virgin Mary).
Photo by W. Castelli, Lübeck.
Copyrights: Lübeck Cathedral Congregation, Endowment of the Cathedral Congregation in the St. Anne's Museum.

118. Aquamanile (Hand basin, probably for warming of water at the fireside). Low German manufacture. Cluny Museum, Paris.
Photo courtesy of Cluny Museum, Paris.

119. Albrecht Dürer (1471-1528) *Abduction on a Unicorn* (also called "The Abduction of Proserpine"), steel engraving. In the first drafts, the seducer's mount is a horse. "By transforming the horse into a fabulous unicorn, evocative of the ideas of night, death and destruction, Dürer invested a violent but perfectly natural scene with an infernal character unparalleled in representations of the subject except for Rembrandt's early picture in Berlin." (Panofsky Erwin, *Albrecht Dürer,* Princeton, 1948, vol. I, p. 196).

120. Comptroller of the Household section of the Netherlands Print Collections, Wild youth (or *hoyden*?) as unicorn jockey, last quarter of fifteenth century. Rijksprentenkabinet, Amsterdam. "Die wilden Leute des Mittelalters," (Medieval Wild Folk) catalog, Hamburg, 1963.
Photo by Foto Marburg.

121. Leonardo da Vinci (1452-1519). Lady with unicorn, pen-and-ink sketch. Oxford (England). In Leonardo's own handling of *Physiologus* (contained in the collection of the "Notebooks and Drawings," Leipzig, 1952) the unicorn is a symbol for licentiousness (*intemperanza*). But is the lady's attitude in the drawing really reproachful in character?
Photo from Ashmolean Museum, Oxford.

122. Israhel van Meckenem (ca. 1450-1503). Joust between man and woman. Copy after the Old Masters "ES" (Master "ES" lived in Konstanz, namely in a region where the wild folk played their pranks). *Israhel van Meckenem, Goldsmith and Copperplate Engraver,* published by the city of Bocholt, 1953.
Photo by Albertina, Vienna.

123. Albrecht Dürer (1471–1528). Unicorn (symbol of darkness) and crane (as symbol of the dawn), after psalm 129 (130). Marginal sketch for Emperor Maximilian's prayer book. Panofsky, Erwin. *Albrecht Dürer,* Princeton, 1948, vol. I, p. 189, erroneously quotes Psalm 80.

124. Upper Rhineland master, end fifteenth century. Two women with unicorns, pen-and-ink drawing.
Photo from Copperplate Engravings Collection of the Public Art Collection, Basel.

125. Unicorn beside a treasure chest, symbolizing the motto *Pretiosum quod utile* (Valuable because of its usefulness). Sambucus, Joannes. *Emblemata,* second edition, 1566, no. 144 – Henkel and Schoene, col. 420.

126. Moretto (1498-1555). St. Justine with unicorn and donor. St. Justine (ca. A.D. 300) was given the unicorn because she had defended her virginity at the price of martyrdom.
Vienna Museum of the History of Art.

126a. St. Stephen's corpse guarded by animals, the eighth of twenty-three Gobelins on Stephen, donated ca. 1500 to Auxerre Cathedral by Bishop Jean Baillet, and now in the Cluny Museum, Paris.
Photo from Cluny Museum, Paris.

127. Linsey-woolsey hanging showing the story of Pyramus and Thisbe. An ancient Near Eastern legend relates that the two lovers came to an understanding through a hole in a wall, trysted on a tomb, were menaced by a lion, and each believing mistakenly that the other had fallen victim to the beast, committed suicide. The story surfaces again in Ovid's *Metamorphoses* and impinges farcically

in Shakespeare's *Midsummer Night's Dream*. Its further development may be due to d'Urfé's novel *Astraea* (cf. illustration 157). Canvasses relating to the story are reminiscent of Renaissance motifs, which lead one strongly to recollect the well in illustration 132. The tree of life is older – if that is referred to here. Thus there is a confluence in late rustic art of various cultural epochs.
Photo from Schleswig-Holstein Provincial Museum, Schleswig.

128. The unicorn expels the venomous snakes from a spring, symbolizing the saying *Nil inexploratus* ("Leave no stone unturned"). Reusener, Nicolas. *Emblemata*, 1581, vol. 2, no. 4, Henkel and Schoene col. 411.

129. Various types of unicorn from Pierre Pomet's pharmaceutical text. To do this author justice, we must admit that he was extremely skeptical as to the existence of the unicorn and the healing power of its horn. The two-horned pirassoipi which he illustrates and describes in company with the unicorn is said to live in Arabia. where its horn also is used for curative purposes. Pomet, Peter. *Honest Grocer and Dry Goods Dealer* (German version of original French *Histoire des Drogues*, Paris, 1694).

130-135. Unicorn hunt, French and Flemish Gobelins ca. 1500, New York. The seventh tapestry of which only a fragment was available has not been illustrated here. Compare the detailed description in the body of the text and p. 201. See also Holm, Edith, *Die Einhornjagd auf den Teppichen der Anne de Bretagne* (The Unicorn Hunt on the Anne of Brittany Tapestries), 1967; Rorimer, James J. *The Unicorn Tapestries at the Cloisters;* fourth edition, 1962; Säizle, Karl. *Tier und Mensch–Gottheit und Dämon* (Beast and Man—Divinity and Demon), 1965. Rorimer's book contains color prints of all seven tapestries.
Photos courtesy of Metropolitan Museum of Art, New York.

136. Unicorn and stag in landscape as alchemical symbols for man's spirit, soul and substance respectively, from the so-called "Lambsprinck" figures. Watercolor painting ca. 1577-1583 in a manuscript by Janus Lacinius.
Hartlaub, G. F. *Der Stein der Weisen* (The Philosophers' Stone), Munich, 1959.
Photo from Germanic National Museum, Nürnberg.

137. Adam in Paradise, Siena, marble intarsia in floor of the St. Catherine's chapel in the Black Friars Church. Mistakenly ascribed to Domenico Baccafumi, probably by Giovanni Battista Sozzini. Also erroneously interpreted as Orpheus or Aesculapius.
Cust, Robert H. Hobart. *The Pavement Masters of Siena*, 1901.
Hartlaub, G. F. *Zauber des Spiegels* (Magic of the Mirror), 9151.
Photo by Alinari, Florence.

138. Lady with unicorn as an amulet for Cardinal Archbishop Charles of Lyons, ca. 1500. Tapestry cartoon. See *Gazette des Beaux Arts*, November 1967, p. 174.
Photo from French National Library, Paris.

139. Detail of wellhead from Neuburg on the Danube. Limestone. ca. 1530.
Photo courtesy of Bavarian National Museum, Munich.

140. Nikolaus Birkenholtz, "Unicorn" flagon of narwhal's tusk, ca. 1600. Grand-ducal Private Collections, Darmstadt.

141. Unicorn as constellation on celestial sphere, by Vincenzo Coronelli, circa 1700. Cologne City Museum.
Photo from Rheinisches Bildarchiv, Cologne.

142. Elieser Susmann, detail of lion and unicorn in wood ceiling of Horb synagogue, 1735. Endowment by Bamber City Art Collection on permanent exhibition in Israel Museum, Jerusalem. Strauss, Heinrich. "Die Horb-Synagoge im Israel-Museum" (Horb Synagogue in the Israel Museum), article in *Ariel* (Jerusalem), no. 9 (Winter 1969). "Monumenta Judaica" catalog, Cologne 1964, No. E 260, cf. E 281 and E 324.
Photo from Rheinisches Bildarchiv, Cologne.

143. Burgundian (?) ornate flagon ca. 1440-1450.
Photo courtesy of History of Art Museum, Vienna.

144. "Unicorn pole" (Narwhal tusk) as sign of the monastery apothecary's store at Rottenbuch, ca. 1750.
Stafski, Hainz. *Aus alten Apotheken* (Gleanings from ancient drugstores), Third ed, Munich, 1961.
Photo from Germanic National Museum, Nürnberg.

145. Mortar from Frankfurt apothecary shop with the otherwise similarly relevant apothecary crest. Historical Museum, Frankfurt am Main, seventeenth century.

146. Unicorn amulet, segment of narwhal tusk in gold mounting from the estate of the Campion of Danny family, ca. 1600. The amulet shows traces of scraping evidently for medical use. In Victoria and Albert Museum, London.
Hansmann and Kriss-Rettenbeck. *Amulett und Talisman* (Amulet and Talisman), Munich, 1966.

147. Ernst Fuchs, *The Begetting of the Unicorn*, copper etching, 1956. The sheet is part of a set titled "The Passion of the Unicorn," expressly allusive to Christ and therefore assimilating the early Christian interpretation of the unicorn.
The Unicorn's Triumph is from the same series.

148. Ernst Fuchs, *The Artist and the Unicorn*, copper etching. "While working on the plate for the scene "In Hades," I clearly imagined the vision of the young unicorn before its horn broke through the forehead. The next plate to that "The Artist and the Unicorn" shows the animal pushing his horn against the artist's temple, while the artist holding a stylus in his hand works on the plate. The unicorn is *my* animal; I was the unicorn within me. The unicorn was *id*, the spirit that was driving me on. I painted it in the greatest variety of phases of its metamorphosis and continued to portray its passion, which I was indeed experiencing in my own life, on the subsequent copper plates." Commentary by Ernst Fuchs in Weis, Helmut and Fuchs, Ernst. *Das graphische Werk* (Graphic Composition), Vienna, 1967.

149. Rosita Salem, Unicorn. This example of "magic realism" shows the legendary animal's horn as a primitive force emerging from the soil, literally *chthonic* (from the earth) and also in the erotic sense corresponding to the unicorn tradition. I owe the reference to this contemporary work of art, as well as a great deal of further assistance to Dr. Alfred Mikesch of Vienna.

150. Gustave Moreau (1826-1896), *Ladies and Unicorns*.
Photo from Gustave Moreau Museum, Paris.

151. Triumph of Innocence. Stained glass window from St. Vincent's Church, Rouen, 1515. Now in Soho Museum, London.

152. Jean Duvet (1485-ca. 1556). Hunting monarch attacked by unicorn. Copperplate engraving from a set of five unicorn scenes, said to allude to the love of Henry II and Diane de Poitiers (cf. illustration 105).
Photo by Albertina, Vienna.

153. Sea Unicorn and Narwhal from Pomet's pharmaceutical text (cf. illustration 129).

154. Advertisement poster of an anonymous London physician in the seventeenth century.
Photo from Bodleian Library, Oxford.

155. Sea unicorn, after the *Carta Marina* (Maritime Chart) of Bishop Olaus Magnus, the Swedish geographer, Venice, 1539.
Brenner, Oscar. *Die achte Karte des Olaus Magnus vom Jahre* 1539 (The authentic 1539 map of Olaus Magnus, after the copy in Munich State Library), Christiania (Oslo), 1886.

156. Watermark from an Innsbruck chancery deed dated 1366 **Briquet, C. M.** *Les Filigranes* (Watermarks), vol. 3, no. 9948, Leipzig, 1923). Briquet's massive manual on watermarks illustrates more than 500 unicorn watermarks; in France alone, this indefatigable collector verified 1133 of these marks.

157. Melchior Lechter (1865-1937), Publisher's house seal, 1908.

158. Melchior Lechter, Title page for book, 1909. Melchior Lechter catalog, Münster, 1965.

159. *La Dame a la Licorne* (Lady with Unicorn), sketch by Jean Cocteau, from the estate of Heinz Rosen who as choreographer directed the original presentation of the *Lady with the Unicorn* ballet in Munich in 1953. Jean Cocteau granted him all the rights to that ballet and the drawings pertaining thereto.

160. Upper Austrian tarot card from deck by Josef Dimler, 1836. In Upper Austrian National Museum, Linz.
"Das Bauernjahr 1969" (Farmer's Annual Calendar for 1969), Linz on the Danube.

161. Augustin de Saint-Aubin (1736-1807), engraving after a drawing by Charles Nicolas Cochin the Younger (1715-1790). The subject of the drawing is an attack on lovers' lane by lions and the defense of the couples by unicorns. It is one of the illustrations to Honoré d'Urfé (1568-1625) pastoral romance *Astraea*. My thanks are due to M. Georges Mongrédion of Paris for these particulars.

Index

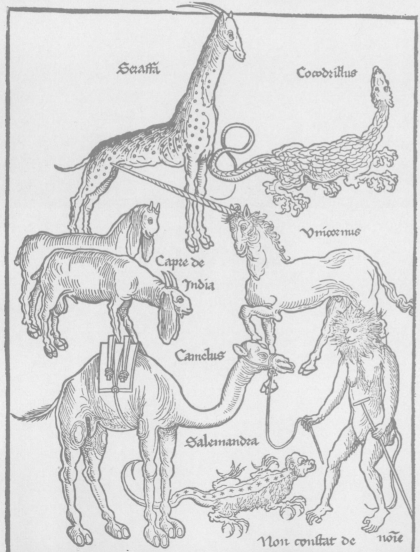

Seraffa

Cocodrillus

Capre de India

Vnicornus

Camelus

Salemandra

Non constat de noie